Social Justice/Criminal Justice

"This is a fascinating, careful, and insightful examination of one of our country's most pressing and persistent problems: How to achieve a decent society and an equitable criminal justice system when both remain shaped by pervasive injustices. Informed by law, philosophy, history and hard data, the book's rigorously-reasoned arguments for reform are must-reading for anyone interested in racial and economic justice."

—Gabriel J. (Jack) Chin *(He/him) 趙健民, Edward L. Barrett Chair and Martin Luther King, Jr. Professor of Law, Director of Clinical Education, University of California at Davis School of Law, USA*

"We have needed a book that addresses the problem of racial injustice without hyperbole or defensiveness. We have needed a book that approaches the pursuit of social justice with data and realism. We have needed a book that informs instead of incites. Heffernan and Zhang have given us that book."

— Todd Clear, *University Distinguished Professor, Rutgers University, USA, and author of* Imprisoning Communities: How Mass Incarceration Makes Disadvantaged Neighborhoods Worse

"Aristotle begins his Politics by distinguishing the ideal state as such from the ideal feasible state, which Aristotle will address. The intellectual challenge of such non-ideal theory for criminal justice is to go the whole route from considering ideal justice (needed to guide practical policies), through consideration of how criminal justice systems actually function, to the feasible improvements that will make such systems just enough (for social systems run by actual humans). Armed with both philosophical understanding of social justice and concrete knowledge of actual criminal justice systems, William Heffernan and Shuhao Zhang take on this challenge in Social Justice/Criminal Justice. The result is a readable and useful recipe for a feasible ideal criminal justice system."

—Jeffrey Reiman, *William Fraser McDowell Professor Emeritus of Philosophy and Public Policy, American University, and author of* The Rich Get Richer and the Poor Get Prison

William C. Heffernan

Social Justice/ Criminal Justice

Race and Class in the Administration of Criminal Law

palgrave
macmillan

William C. Heffernan
John Jay College of Criminal Justice
City University of New York
New York, USA

With Contrib. by
Shuhao Zhang
University of Maryland
College Park, MD, USA

ISBN 978-3-031-75396-1 ISBN 978-3-031-75397-8 (eBook)
https://doi.org/10.1007/978-3-031-75397-8

This Palgrave Macmillan imprint is published by the registered company Springer Nature Switzerland AG
The registered company address is: Gewerbestrasse 11, 6330 Cham, Switzerland

Introduction

Introduction: Mandela's Role Reversal At the beginning of the 1963 trial that would lead to his 27-year imprisonment by the government of the Union of South Africa, Nelson Mandela was asked by the clerk of the court to enter a plea. The clerk's question, a standard one at criminal trials, provoked an unusual answer. "It is not I, but the government, that should be in the dock," Mandela stated. "I plead not guilty."

The government as the guilty party? Mandela didn't simply deny guilt, he also reversed roles, saying that South Africa's government "should be in the dock." Mandela was a political prisoner, of course. The charges against him centered on his efforts to end apartheid. They were concerned with structural injustice, in other words, and Mandela's two-sentence reply parried the charges brought against him by claiming that the government was using the legal system to perpetuate its wrongful practices. Given the special nature of the case against him, someone might say that Mandela's response, while jarring, was a limited one—that it concerned a form of unjust political oppression, not a form of unjust social oppression generally. But while this is a possible reading of Mandela's 1963 plea when it's considered on a stand-alone basis, remarks he delivered on a later occasion unmistakably establish that his role reversal was intended to indict the entire framework of apartheid (and not merely the constitutional arrangements that sustained it), for he also stated more generally that the law "as it is written and designed by our nationalist government [i.e., the one that adopted the apartheid laws that were the subject of his 1963 trial] is law which, in our view, is intolerable, unjust, and immoral." In the Union of South Africa, in other words, criminal law was an instrument of oppression, not a social good.

Did Mandela mean by this that, prior to the establishment of the Republic of South Africa, *all* criminal proceedings—even those cases brought against Afrikaners for harming other Afrikaners, and even those cases (rarely) brought against Afrikaners for harming non-whites—were illegitimate? And, in extending Mandela's remarks beyond South Africa, might one say consistently with his premises that criminal law operates as a means of oppression regardless of locale when government brings criminal charges against someone whose social misfortunes could have been rectified by government initiatives that reorder the distribution of goods and services? In other words, does social justice take precedence—across-the-board precedence—over criminal justice? Does it only sometimes merit this precedence? Or, does it perhaps never merit this given the social function of criminal law?

Mandela's remarks merely suggest the importance of these general questions. Neither Mandela the liberationist lawyer of 1963 nor Mandela the political leader of the 1990s can reasonably have been expected to address systematically the issues at stake or the numerous subsidiary ones that follow from them. The questions are inescapably important, though, not just in the context of South African life but because they're pertinent in any setting where some citizens live under conditions of material privation and where these citizens are charged with crimes by a government that might have—but hasn't—taken steps to bring that privation to an end. They're priority questions, in other words, questions about the relative importance of social justice and criminal justice. They allow for the possibility of criminal justice in settings where social justice is *not* at issue. But they focus attention on issues of precedence when social justice *is* at issue, for when this is the case, Mandela's point about the law's function as an instrument of subjection can't be disregarded.

This book considers the priority issues implicit in Mandela's plea. Its informing premise is that there are sometimes antinomies within the concept of justice itself. In following standard accounts of the term, we can say that *justice* refers to the fair terms of cooperation free and equal individuals would adopt for living together. Standard accounts often fail to address tensions that arise between different types of justice, however. hey avoid this by presupposing an *ideal society*, one in which no one violates the obligations of restraint essential to communal life—and thus by setting aside questions of non-ideal theory and focusing exclusively on how idealized individuals would behave.

If, in contrast, it's assumed, first, that it's worthwhile to rely on ideal theory to identify the key features of social justice but, second, that communal life will sometimes be undermined by acts that violate the obligations of restraint essential to ongoing social relations, then it becomes necessary to turn to non-ideal theory to consider the just resolution of grievances arising from these wrongful acts. On this different, and more realistic, approach to the concept of justice, ideal and non-ideal theory are complementary, for "charges of injustice presuppose ideals of justice," as Tommie Shelby puts it. In adopting this approach, someone points out that claims about the just resolution of grievances—claims about corrective and criminal justice, for instance—unfold against a vision of ideal theory, one in which communal life in its imperfect form is reconciled with a fuller, more satisfactory version of it

Needless to say, once we reason in terms of a contrast between ideal and non-ideal approaches to justice, we have to turn away from utopian conceptions of the subject. The book that follows employs a non-utopian framework, one that relies on three theses for thinking about the social justice/criminal justice connection. The first thesis is concerned with the complementarity of the two types of justice. In focusing on complementarity, someone maintains that social justice is understandable in terms of obligations of reciprocal support and that criminal justice is understandable in terms of obligations of restraint. One can of course imagine social justice without criminal justice. John Rawls actually does so; he calls his project "realistically utopian." On the other hand, the argument developed here outlines the possibility of a non-utopian, decent society, one in which crime continues to occur and a central enforcement agency—i.e., the state—holds people accountable for it. The complementarity thesis holds that the deterrent threat of being held accountable for violating core obligations of restraint reinforces the foundations of communal life. It further holds that, on balance, provision of social justice promotes the possibility of individual adherence to the law.

The second thesis—the *systemic injustice thesis*—is concerned with the converse of this last point. This is that the state has sometimes used its punitive power to reinforce social *in*justice. Mandela's role reversal addressed this phenomenon. The Jim Crow south was also organized around it. In each case, legal rules openly aimed at perpetuating the subordinate position of one social group to another. Even after formal rejection of discriminatory rules, the *vestiges* of systemic injustice may remain critically important in any given society, for the aftereffects of injustice can be felt in the operation of public institutions and in patterns of everyday practice long after the legal authorization of injustice has been rejected. The currently advantaged may continue to accumulate advantages, in other words, even under laws that are framed in formally neutral terms.

The third thesis—the *superfluousness thesis*—is concerned with a drastic remedy for the vestiges of the past. In responding to the vestiges problem, someone might conceivably argue that social justice, once achieved, will make criminal justice unnecessary: that violations of the obligations of restraint will no longer be a threat to the social order once the state provides its citizens with the full requisites of social justice. Well, maybe. There certainly are compelling data points to cite in favor of *less* punishment and *less* massed force by the current legal system. On the other hand, it's clearly imprudent to take literally—or even semi-literally—slogans such as *defund the police* or *prison abolition*. How are these to be applied, one wonders, in the event of a string of violent rapes in a neighborhood, or in cases where motorists speed substantially above posted limits, thereby killing pedestrians at intersections, or in the face of persistent tax evasion? The sounder approach is non-utopian. It is to build a just social order but to plan, in the meantime, for continued operation of a humane central enforcement agency that promotes the possibility of cooperative activity.

The chapters that follow develop these theses in roughly the order in which they've been presented. The first section relies on the complementarity thesis to outline the key features of the two dimensions of justice mentioned in the book's title. It treats *justice* as the term essential to both the distribution of communal wealth and the exercise of coercive power since each is concerned with the fair exercise of power over others to promote collective life.

The second section addresses the other two theses. Its opening chapter is concerned with the dystopian possibility that state power—in particular, the power to punish—will be used to entrench social injustice. This power may be deployed openly (as in the case of apartheid and Jim Crow). Alternatively, it may be deployed through reliance on genuinely neutral laws that reinforce patterns of previously legalized injustice, in which case the vestiges of the past continue to figure prominently in current life.

The other chapter in the second section considers a utopian response to this dystopian possibility—that achievement of social justice will make criminal justice unnecessary. In rejecting this thesis, we set the stage for the remaining sections of the book. That is, we forgo the tantalizing utopian argument for dispensing with a central enforcement agency and begin investigating the actual administration of criminal law—in particular, its impact on race and class—in advanced industrial societies as they respond to the vestiges of social injustice.

The final two sections carry out this investigation by means of a straightforward division of labor, with the third section focusing on vestiges of the past that continue to plague internal the administration of criminal law, and the fourth on proactive changes in social structure that can positively affect its administration. Chapters in the third section presuppose a commitment by law enforcement professionals (not merely police but also prosecutors and judges) to genuinely race- and class-neutral exercises of discretion in applying laws that are already race- and class-neutral on their face. Chapters in the final section presuppose a society-wide commitment to eliminating the vestiges of past injustice. They presuppose active government measures, not merely prohibitions on discrimination, measures that address the disadvantages of the least advantaged members of society. Taken together, the two sections offer a realistic way to build a decent society. They don't assume the possibility of a crime-free utopia. They do, however, suggest how social justice can make the administration of criminal law more humane—and, in the process, reduce reliance on it.

Contents

List of Tables

PART I

Theory: Two Dimensions of Justice

CHAPTER 1

Criminal Justice

The criminal process begins with an act of domination, one in which an agent of the state deprives someone of his/her freedom of movement by means of an arrest. Arrest is typically followed by an act of submission. That is, a suspect's usual response to an arrest is to acquiesce to the show of authority by the official making it. If submission is the outcome, subsequent events are defined by a dynamic of mastery and compliance. The mastery at stake is both physical and psychological—physical because the suspect's freedom of movement is determined by someone else and psychological because the arrestee realizes that, for the duration of confinement, compliance defines the terms of the relationship with his/her captors.

If submission is *not* the outcome of an arrest, the quest for domination becomes even more intense. Mere mastery not having been achieved, the arresting officer is authorized to escalate the use of force—up to and including deadly force in some circumstances—in order to secure submission to his/her authority. Mastery is the aim of an arrest, in other words, and if mastery isn't secured by a show of authority, extra force may be employed to ensure that a suspect will, ultimately, comply with an officer's show of authority.

Because these points are descriptively sound, they give rise to a question about justice—i.e., whether an arrest based on probable cause for an illegal act can be characterized as an act of *just* domination. That is, if

W. C. Heffernan, *Social Justice/Criminal Justice*,
https://doi.org/10.1007/978-3-031-75397-8_1

we define *criminal justice* as the term that refers to the process of state-initiated demand for accountability with respect to an allegation of legally prohibited wrongful force or fraud, we have to agree that the notion of just domination is a key component of all stages of the criminal process. Arresting a suspect amounts to an act of domination. Condemning a convicted defendant following his conviction amounts to a further act of domination (for only a masochist would agree to submit to condemnatory comments concerning his/her behavior). And incarcerating someone following conviction also amounts to yet another act of domination (for, again, only a masochist would agree to substantial curtailment of freedom of movement). As noted in the introduction, the term *justice* refers to the conditions free and equal people would adopt for undertaking mutually beneficial activity.[1] *Criminal* justice is different: it's concerned with the conditions in which *un*free and *un*equal people are called on to account for their behavior and, sometimes, are subject to censure and punitive isolation.

At a minimum, then, there's an air of paradox associated with criminal justice. Indeed, it might even be said that the concept of criminal justice turns the notion of justice inside out, for criminal justice operates by means of domination whereas the more general concept of justice is concerned with the possibility of cooperation among free and equal people.

The seeming paradox can be dispelled, though, if we return to the suggestion, contained in the introduction, that ideal and non-ideal theories offer complementary ways to think about the concept of justice. Once the possibility of complementarity is borne in mind, one can see that the fair terms of cooperation (identified by means of ideal theory) are the defining feature of justice, and that domination is the exception, with the conditions of just domination (identified by means of non-ideal theory) deemed acceptable only because these conditions may be necessary to sustain an ongoing scheme of fair cooperation.

Furthermore, it's also essential to bear a related point in mind—that even when domination is legitimate, the risk remains that it may shade into oppression. Indeed, because sporadic acts of oppression by officials of the state sometimes morph into systemic oppression, it must be realized (as per the Mandela challenge) that the term *criminal justice* may serve as a mask for state-imposed injustice—and state-imposed injustice is of course a far more serious threat than are sporadic incidents of injustice carried out by rogue officials of the state.

These are the theses that will be developed in the following chapters. Because the inquiry is set in motion by examining the mastery/submission dynamic, its starting point for reasoning about the criminal law is that there must be a clear-eyed acknowledgment of the risks associated with the exercise of coercive power. As against this, the thesis affirms the need for a centralized agency that has the authority to hold people accountable for violating the fair terms of communal life. The justification for this thesis is divided into three parts. The first is concerned with obligations of restraint essential to an ongoing scheme of cooperation, the second with the state's monopoly power in addressing violations of these obligations, and the third with the possibility that the state will use its monopoly power unjustly. The three sections are part of a unified whole. When considered together, they affirm the following: that it's justifiable, *at least in principle*, for an appropriately constrained central enforcement agency (i.e., the state) to exercise coercive power impartially in the course of overseeing each person's obligation to exercise restraint in dealing with others.

Obligations of Restraint

If *justice* functions as the master concept for thinking about the fair terms of social cooperation, then the rationale for a system of state domination of suspects can only be the contribution this makes to ensuring fidelity to those terms. To assess this claim, we should begin by considering a precondition for cooperation: adherence to obligations of restraint concerning (i) the use of wrongful force and (ii) the use of fraud. The next chapter considers a different set of obligations essential to justice, those of mutual support. We start, though, with the rationale for the two kinds of obligations of restraint just mentioned.

Consider first the issue of wrongful force—not force *simpliciter*, for there are occasions when individuals may justifiably use force to defend themselves and others, but rather force that cannot properly be used against others. The outer boundaries of the term *wrongful force* are contestable. Its core is easily identified, though, for this is understandable in terms of unprovoked acts of aggression (murder, rape, assault, and robbery, for example) that deprive people of their physical well-being when these people pose no immediate threat to others. The wrongful force obligation is understandable in terms of a prohibition of domination: it's concerned with acts that directly interfere with an individual's capacity to engage others voluntarily in cooperative activity.

The second subject area of the obligations of restraint has to do with fraud. Here, as before, the outer limits of the prohibition are contestable while the prohibition's core is easily identified, for fraud consists of a deliberate effort by one party to secure an advantage over another by means of deception. Unlike wrongful force, fraud isn't understandable in terms of direct domination. It's *in*directly concerned with this, though, for the premise of a fraud prohibition is that it shields each individual from acts he or she otherwise wouldn't undertake.

Taken together, these two subject areas of the obligations of restraint can be grouped under the heading *WFF*—i.e., wrongful force and fraud. Although they are concerned with different kinds of acts, all *WFF* prohibitions are defined by a negative obligation of general scope: by a duty to respect each person's interest in making independent decisions for him- or herself. Each person's adherence to this duty is a precondition to maintenance of the fair terms of communal life. It's by bearing this obligation in mind that we can understand the complementarity of ideal and non-ideal theory when thinking about justice.

In what sense are *WFF* prohibitions obligations of justice? They are, of course, obligations enforced by the law. The legal status of these prohibitions isn't what makes them obligations of justice, however. On the contrary, a criminal code that contains *WFF* prohibitions *affirms* their status as obligations of justice, for law can't create justice, though it can recognize and enforce what is already just. Fidelity to *WFF* prohibitions is itself just. It isn't simply a precondition of justice, though it certainly comes under this heading since cooperative activity is impossible without it. But fidelity to prohibitions of *WFF* is also just in itself, *and adherence to these prohibitions is binding even on people who don't acknowledge them as obligatory*, for in affirming them as duties, one also affirms respect for the equal freedom of others—and, in denying them someone rejects adherence to the requirements of justice.

We will turn next to enforcement questions related to the obligations to refrain from *WFF*. Before doing so, however, we should note an important feature of these obligations that's unrelated to government's enforcement power—i.e., that, apart from the prospect of government force, an expectation of a *reciprocity of restraint* often prompts people to honor their obligations to others.[2] Communal life is facilitated by this expectation; it's facilitated, in other words, by each person's willingness to exercise forbearance in his/her dealings with others in expectation of the forbearance others will exercise as well. It's because this is so that we can say the obligations of restraint are supplemented by a reciprocity of restraint. It's essential to begin, then, with a claim about individual obligation—essential to begin by claiming that each person owes others obligations of restraint with respect to *WFF*. However, it's helpful to supplement this claim with the observation that long-term stability in communal life hinges on the confidence others entertain that others will reciprocally honor the obligations of restraint.

Bringing in the State

And what if the reciprocity of restraint breaks down in a given community? What if one person intentionally attacks another? What if people lose their life savings because someone has defrauded them? These questions have an obvious answer, it might be said: bring in the state. That is, design a legal system that will hold people accountable for acts that inflict serious harm; vest that system with preclusive authority to call people to account for this harm, thereby forestalling retaliatory violence; train officials to exercise coercive power impartially; and contend that, provided they do so, there is no paradox in the term *just domination*, for the legal system then responds appropriately to one of the tragic features of the human condition—each person's capacity to harm others.

We can call this the *criminal justice option* when thinking about the appropriate response to violations of the obligations of restraint. It's the option that will be defended in the remainder of the chapter—and, at greater length, throughout the book. Before turning to this, though, we should examine a forerunner of criminal justice: *lex talionis*, a framework that authorizes *victims* to initiate retaliation as a form of grievance-redress. *Lex talionis* (the law of the talion) is endorsed in two books of the *Torah*, *Exodus* and *Leviticus*. Because it appears in the Bible, many premodern readers assumed that it has a unique connection to the law of the Israelites. Research has now established, however, that what Moses announced actually had been included in an earlier Middle Eastern set of laws, the Code of Hammurabi.[3] Though intriguing, this point is of no significance for our purposes. What matters for us is that *lex talionis* stands as an alternative to criminal justice while nonetheless addressing questions of fairness when dealing with grievance-redress.

Leviticus contains the following version of *lex talionis*, a version it attributes to Moses:

> Anyone who kills a human being shall be put to death. Anyone who kills an animal shall make restitution for it, life for life. Anyone who maims another shall suffer the same injury in return: fracture for fracture, eye for eye, tooth for tooth; the injury inflicted is the injury to be suffered.[4]

Given its emphasis on equivalence, *lex talionis* shows an unmistakable concern with fairness in the resolution of grievances. But given its silence concerning culpability, *lex talionis* can't be said to deal satisfactorily with questions of justice when someone has been harmed. Moreover, given its reliance on victim-initiated retaliation, *lex talionis* can't be classified as an example of criminal justice. Rather, it must instead be viewed as a pre-state framework of grievance-redress and harm-prevention, one that holds out the possibility of victim satisfaction for harm suffered plus (general and specific) deterrence without relying on a central enforcement agency to uphold the obligations of restraint. Each of these points merits further consideration if we are to understand the distinctive features of criminal justice.

Think first about the importance of equivalence. *Life-for-life* figures twice in the passage just quoted; other types of equivalence (*eye for eye, tooth for tooth*, for instance) also appear in it. *Life-for-life* is prescribed for the loss of *human* life. It's also prescribed for the loss of *animal* life, though in the latter case only as a form of restitutionary exchange while in the former as a type of sacrifice (as in, *your family member is to be sacrificed for the loss suffered by my family member*). Because the passage concludes with a generalization about *the injury inflicted*, it unmistakably holds that fairness hinges on equivalence between what was lost and what is to be forgone. The passage's informing principle is negative reciprocity, in other words. Positive reciprocity consists of an exchange of equal value. Negative reciprocity consists of equivalent loss. Fairness is at stake in both types of reciprocity, the passage implies.

Does this insistence on equivalence meet the standards of justice? The answer is *no*. This is because *lex talionis*, when understood simply in terms of *x for x*, doesn't deal with questions of culpability. Did *B* intentionally kill *A*? Did *B* negligently kill *A*? Did *B* kill *A* in self-defense? The culpability issues essential to each of these questions are inescapable as far as justice is concerned. *Lex talionis* doesn't address them, though.[5]

Moreover, it's incapable of addressing them, for its concern is equivalent harm, not the culpability of the person who brings about harm. To put this point differently, if we imagine a different framework, one in which the disposition of the actor causing harm is taken into account (intention vs. negligence, and intention to cause harm once justified self-defense is considered), we then have to abandon the harm-for-harm equivalence that informs negative reciprocity. Instead, we have to consider a framework in which a balance is struck between resulting harm, on the one hand, and the disposition of the person causing harm, on the other. Justice requires this refinement of the negative reciprocity framework. When reasoning in terms of justice, someone takes into account the equivalence consideration essential to *lex talionis*. A commitment to justice profoundly alters that framework, however, because it requires consideration of culpability as well.

And of course, *criminal* justice relies on an institutional apparatus that is entirely missing in *lex talionis*. Under *lex talionis*, victims hold offenders accountable for violations of the obligations of restraint. Institutions charged with enforcement of these obligations aren't involved. *Lex talionis* does of course place a ceiling on grievance-redress (one eye, not two eyes, when only a single eye has been lost), but it says nothing about the procedures victims must follow to ensure that accountability is fairly imposed, nor does it say anything about how this ceiling will be enforced in the event that a victim exceeds it when seeking revenge.

This is exactly what criminal justice provides—that is, criminal justice is administered by means of state-based institutions that hold individuals accountable for the harm they've brought about. Given this general point, we can now appreciate the distinction between *lex talionis* and what was introduced earlier as the *criminal justice option*. Of the four features of this option, the first is the most straightforward: criminal justice is the backstop for shortcomings in the reciprocity of restraint. This is a point of sociological and legal significance—*sociological* because the state speaks for the community in enforcing prohibitions against *WFF* and *legal* in that the mode of enforcement relies on coercive power. With criminal justice, a third-party perspective supersedes that of the second party. That is, instead of authorizing aggrieved parties to determine whether they've been wronged, criminal justice authorizes state officials to resolve this question by inquiring into the circumstances of harm in a given instance. We will return in a later chapter to the significance of holding someone to account for possible wrongdoing, for as will be seen even when punishment isn't imposed, it still makes sense to speak of criminal justice in settings when state officials call on someone to account for his/her acts in the wake of a charge of wrongdoing.

The second feature of the criminal justice option is closely related to this, for state officials exercise preclusive authority (i.e., compulsory jurisdiction) in resolving questions about wrongdoing. Because *lex talionis* authorizes aggrieved parties to retaliate for the harm they've suffered, it can lead to a cycle of retaliatory revenge. In precluding victim-initiated retaliation for harm suffered, criminal justice reduces dramatically the possibility of a cycle of violence and therefore holds out the prospect of substantially more deterrence than *lex talionis*. This is because the criminal justice option discourages violence not only when a grievance is upheld as valid but also when one is deemed invalid, for even when government officials refuse to pursue a grievance the aggrieved party is barred from striking back. Max Weber's definition of the state focuses on exactly this point. The state, Weber argues, "is a human community that (successfully) claims *the monopoly of legitimate use of physical force* within a given territory."[6] On this reckoning, compulsory jurisdiction is a defining feature of criminal justice. The state deflects grievance: it uses its monopoly power to channel grievance-redress through institutional pathways, warding off retaliatory violence by prohibiting victims from striking back and requiring alleged offenders to submit to its jurisdiction. In contrast, *lex talionis* has the potential to exacerbate grievance through its authorization of victim-initiated retaliatory harm.

Is a monopoly of legitimate violence a sufficient condition for criminal justice? The answer to this is *no*, for a state that secures this monopoly for itself may, or may not, deploy its power justly. After all, only a moment's thought is needed to establish that government may use its power to perpetuate social *in*justice. This issue will be examined at length in Chapter 3, for it is one of the central features of the social justice/criminal justice connection. All that needs to be noted here is that governments have used their coercive penal power to protect institutions such as slavery (for example, by making it a crime for a slave to escape from his/her master) or the patriarchal family (for example, by exempting husbands from criminal liability for sexually assaulting their wives). The state's monopoly power may have the beneficial effect of forestalling cycles of violent retaliation, in other words, but that power can be justified—can be deemed *just*—only if it is used to enforce impartially the obligations of restraint.

The criminal justice option, we thus can say, offers a justification for the state's power to preclude retaliatory violence if and only if its second component (which is concerned with the contribution to social stability made by the state's monopoly of power) is linked to its third component (which is concerned with the just resolution of grievances). On this reckoning, the criminal justice option hinges on a pragmatic bet. In placing this bet, someone assumes that social peace is dramatically enhanced by a central enforcement agency's successful assertion of the power to preclude retaliatory violence. The bet pays off, someone defending the option would say, only if the monopoly power exercised by the state promotes impartial enforcement of the obligations of restraint.

It's possible to restate the point just made by invoking the social contract framework often used to assess the legitimacy of public institutions. No rationally self-interested individual committed to cooperative activity based on equal respect for others would agree to grant a monopoly of legitimate violence to a central enforcement agency (i.e., the state) absent a reasonably verifiable assurance that this monopoly will be used impartially to vindicate core obligations of restraint. In his *Second Treatise on Civil Government*, John Locke appears to have suggested that an actual contract was adopted to this effect sometime in the distant past.[7] In modifying Locke, we can set aside the fiction of an actual contract and speak instead of a *hypothetical* contract that sets the terms for criminal justice. Clearly, there was never a moment in time when people bargained over the framework for enforcing the obligations of restraint. But because state institutions have developed over centuries and must be assessed by the generations that have inherited them, we can reason in terms of a two-stage thought experiment that leads to adoption of the criminal justice option. In the first stage, rational bargainers unaware of their specific circumstances (and thus uncertain whether they would be weak or strong, rich or poor) agree to grant a central enforcement agency preclusive power to resolve grievances. In the second stage, they would ask about justice, for they would conclude that this preclusive power is subject to abuse unless limited by a requirement that grievances are resolved impartially. In combining the two stages, we might say that no rational bargainer would agree to the creation of institutions with the far-ranging coercive power of courts, police, and corrections *unless* constraints of justice limit the operation of those institutions.[8]

This revision of social contract theory—a revision that moves from the fiction of an actual contract that granted the state a monopoly of legitimate violence to a thought experiment that holds rational bargainers unaware of their specific circumstances would agree to this on the condition of a just exercise of power in enforcing prohibitions on *WFF*—lays the foundation for the criminal justice option outlined at the beginning of this section of the chapter. The revision explains in principle why a central enforcement agency is preferable to a framework of communally authorized retaliation. It doesn't go beyond this. In particular, because the criminal justice option is concerned with principle, not practice, it doesn't suggest that the *actual* legal system delivers just outcomes in resolving grievances. The option outlined above does, however, provide an evaluative standard, one that can be used to assess the legitimacy of decisions by state officials that hold people accountable for the harm they've done others. On this reckoning, criminal justice is indeed a genuine component of justice. Or, to put the point more cautiously, the state's exercise of monopoly power (in particular, its use of dominant force in holding people to account for the harm they've caused) is compatible with the principles of justice *as long as* this power is exercised in a way that sustains the fair terms of cooperation among free and equal people. It would have been risible, in other words, to say that the legal system Mandela confronted in 1963 produced *criminal justice*. It's possible, however, to imagine genuine criminal justice when the state's coercive power is deployed to promote a fair scheme of cooperative activity compatible with social justice.

Restraining the State

What limits should be placed on the state's monopoly power? This is a key question—arguably, *the* key question given the possibility of pathological deployment of state authority—that must be considered when thinking about criminal justice. It's a question that extends beyond constitutions, for the restrictions constitutions place on the state's exercise of power are insufficient to ensure the just resolution of grievances. The chapters in the latter half of the book address issues of justice that go beyond current constitutional law, issues that might lead to the formulation of further constitutional restraints if courts were to show greater sensitivity to racial and class disparities when addressing criminal appeals, and also structural issues related to state capture that defy constitutional interpretation but that are critical to the fair administration of the law. Here, we turn to constitutions themselves, for constitutions must be the starting point for restraining the state's monopoly power.

A constitution has two functions: to establish procedures for the exercise of state power and to set limits on the power exercised. Clearly, the first function has ramifications for the second. That is, in establishing rules for the operation of government, a constitution implicitly sets limits on the reach of government authority. This implicit limitation is insufficient, however, given the threat to personal liberty posed by the state's monopoly of power. Thus, explicit limits—limits that are textually defined—are needed as well. The text of the United States Constitution illustrates the connection between the two functions. On the one hand, it contains numerous provisions that govern the operation of government. Standing alone, these provisions suggest, at least implicitly, what government *may not* do, but the implicit is made explicit in the Bill of Rights, for each of the first eight amendments explicitly restricts government power by identifying rights individuals may assert *against* the state.[9]

Not every provision in the Bill of Rights is indispensable to criminal justice. Many are essential, though, in particular those that challenge the government to justify its exercise of dominant power over an individual and those that mandate equal treatment whenever the government deploys its power. The first of these categories is best approached by reasoning in terms of calibrated levels of scrutiny of government restraints on freedom. The Fourth Amendment authorizes modest restrictions on liberty interests.[10] In particular, it is held to require articulable suspicion for brief stops but probable cause for arrests.[11] More exacting scrutiny is required for conviction at trial—i.e., proof beyond a reasonable doubt. Even more scrutiny is implicit in the prohibition on cruel and unusual punishments (although this point isn't established in the case law that interprets the Eighth Amendment), for the Eighth Amendment's use of the word *cruel* appears to require a persuasive justification for any sentence since this is accompanied by condemnation of the conduct for which the sentence is imposed.[12]

In addition to these calibrated principles bearing on domination and submission, another one is essential, a principle that requires similar treatment of similar cases. This of course is an indispensable general principle of justice. The textual basis for it is to be found in the Fourteenth Amendment provision that prohibits denial of *equal protection of the laws*, a phrase with relevance to matters unrelated to the administration of criminal law, but that's unmistakably pertinent to it as well.[13]

*

This chapter has addressed the following question: if the criminal process unfolds through acts of domination by state officials, in what sense can there be criminal *justice*? Its answer can be summarized in the following three sentences. First, the word *justice* functions as the master concept for thinking about the fair terms of cooperation between free and equal people. But second, the criminal law relies on a series of steps that *deny* people their freedom, thus jeopardizing a key component of justice. So third, criminal justice is provided only when state officials impartially determine that a suspect has violated the obligations of restraint essential to collective life, for when this standard is met the law affirms the overriding importance of the cooperative activity in a free society.

When considered together, these propositions suggest something disquieting—that criminal justice risks *in*justice to achieve justice. The deprivation of freedom essential to the operation of criminal law may have no connection to social justice. After all, the rich may be punished as well as the poor; the privileged may be imprisoned as well as those who are underprivileged. But if criminal law is applied in ways that disproportionately deny freedom to the disadvantaged, it can perpetuate—and perhaps even worsen—social injustice. This is the book's core concern. To examine it properly, we should turn to the paired concepts of *social justice* and *social injustice*.

Notes

1. For elaboration on this characterization of justice, see Rawls, *supra* note 3 in Introduction.
2. No commentator appears to have used the phrase *reciprocity of restraint* in commenting on the obligations discussed here. For discussion of this kind of reciprocity in the context of modern warfare, see Robert Axelrod, *The Evolution of Cooperation* 83 (1984).
3. See W.W. Davies, *Codes of Hammurabi and Moses* (1905).
4. *Leviticus* 24: 18–21 (New Revised Standard Version 2007).
5. The issue of unintentional homicide is addressed elsewhere in the *Torah*. See *Numbers* 35: 22, which expressly prohibits execution for this. The life-for-life passage in *Leviticus* quoted in the text does

not, however, distinguish between intentional and unintentional homicide.

6. Max Weber, "Politics as a Vocation" [1919], in H.H. Gerth and C. Wright Mills, eds., *From Max Weber* 78 (1956) (emphasis in original).
7. John Locke, *An Essay Concerning the True Original, Extent, and End of Civil Government*, Sects. 11–13 (1690).
8. This argument relies on Rawls's veil-of-ignorance contractualist framework. On Rawls's own analysis, that framework modifies Lockean social contract theory. See Rawls, *supra* note 3 in Introduction at 10. Although this passage refers to social contract theory, Rawls doesn't comment one on the relevance of his framework for thinking about criminal justice. It's because Rawls doesn't systematically address questions about the just treatment of wrongdoing in a socially just society (though he does comment on this in passing in id. at 276–77), that I use the term *decent society*, one that he doesn't employ, to discuss the complementary relationship between social justice and criminal justice in a properly constituted society. Rawls, in contrast, appears to anticipate something more ambitious, for he states that he charts out the preconditions of what he calls a "realistically utopian" political community. See Rawls, *supra* note 7 in Introduction.
9. What follows is a discussion of constitutional limitations that regulate state domination of those subject to the state's coercive authority. The discussion is compatible in a general sense with republicanism's emphasis on non-domination (see, e.g., Philip Pettit, *Republicanism: A Theory of Freedom and Government*, 1997). It is grounded more directly, though, non-ideal liberal political theory—in limited, rule-governed exceptions to the liberal ideal that treats individual adults as free and equal agents.
10. The Fourth Amendment prohibits unreasonable searches and seizures. U.S. Constitution, Amendment IV.
11. See *Terry v. Ohio*, 392 U.S. 1 (1968).
12. The Eighth Amendment provides: "… nor shall cruel and unusual punishments [be] inflicted." U.S. Constitution, Amendment VIII.
13. The Fourteenth Amendment provides: "… nor shall any State … deny any person within its jurisdiction the equal protection of the laws." U.S. Constitution, Amendment XIV, Sect. 1.

CHAPTER 2

Social Justice

Of the paired concepts just mentioned (*social justice* and *social injustice*), the latter serves as an easier starting point for inquiry than the former, for governments have often used their penal power to ensure *un*equal access to communal resources. This, of course, is the premise essential to Mandela's role reversal, and given the universal significance of his comments at the 1963 trial, one can readily identify a *negative* connection—the basis for the systemic injustice thesis—between the two concepts of justice, one in which the position of disadvantaged members of society is worsened through the exercise of state penal power.

The systemic injustice thesis alerts us to the dystopian version of the social justice/criminal justice connection. It's unmistakably important in itself, for in thinking about it we can see how the domination essential to the operation of criminal law has been used to reinforce social injustice. A further question should be posed, though, one that takes us beyond the negative features of the social justice/criminal justice connection by asking whether there is a positive reason to think about the relationship between the two types of justice.

This chapter argues that there is such a reason. It does so by suggesting that a decent society is one where social justice and criminal justice complement each other. As I use the term, the institutions of a decent society provide the requisites of criminal justice *and* social justice. When this is the case, acts of wrongful force and fraud (*WFF*) become less

W. C. Heffernan, *Social Justice/Criminal Justice*,
https://doi.org/10.1007/978-3-031-75397-8_2

frequent as a result of the provision of social justice: the achievement of social justice lessens (even if it doesn't eliminate) the need for criminal justice. This is the positive version of the social justice/criminal justice connection that informs the argument advanced throughout the book. To grasp its significance, we must set aside for a moment the concept of social injustice and instead examine its converse—social justice.

Two Preliminary Issues

To think systematically about social justice, two preliminary issues should be considered. The first is concerned with a problem of definition, the second with a question about the obligations of support associated with the definition that's been provided. As for the first, it's clear that *social justice* is used in many different senses. Each of these general senses is concerned, in one way or another, with egalitarianism—i.e., with an overall orientation that insists on the equal worth and dignity of every person within a polity. Consistently with this, and somewhat more specifically, *social justice* is used to discuss government measures designed to overcome inequalities of birth: it focuses on initiatives designed to mitigate the birth lottery, in other words, and so to promote the possibility of equality of opportunity. In its modest form, *social justice* refers only to this; that is, the term is used to refer to measures designed to ensure fair equality of opportunity for everyone within a given community. In its more ambitious form, social justice refers to something more—to initiatives that ensure equality in the distribution of wealth. The remarks that follow defend the less ambitious version of social justice. As a definitional matter, they treat *social justice* as the concept that refers to government-sponsored efforts that aim at ensuring fair equality of opportunity for all members of a given society.

This definitional point sets the stage for a second question about social justice, for someone might ask *why* he or she has an obligation to contribute to efforts that seek to overcome the disadvantages of another person's birth. Prohibitions on *WFF* are indeed universally binding, a skeptic taking this position might say, so each person has an obligation of restraint vis-a-vis others; and the state is properly charged with enforcing obligations of restraint against those who refuse to honor them. But what rationale, the skeptic would add, can be advanced on behalf of *further* obligations—i.e., obligations of support that aim at correcting disadvantages attributable to the circumstances of birth? However unfortunate these circumstances may be, justice doesn't require those who are more advantaged to take corrective measures with respect to them. To put this point differently, a skeptic would say: (i) a state committed to justice must enforce obligations of restraint concerning *WFF*, (ii) it must do so even with respect to people who refuse to acknowledge these obligations as binding, but (iii) it must enforce further obligations only when people *voluntarily* assume these by engaging in productive exchange with one another.

We can call this the *minimalist* conception of justice. It has often been supported by commentators in the Anglo-American tradition. Two centuries ago, Lord Melbourne defended the general principles associated with minimalism when, as prime minister, he remarked that "[t]he whole duty of government is to prevent crime and to preserve contracts."[1] Contemporary commentators have expanded on Melbourne's pithy statement. Robert Nozick contends, for instance, that "taxation of earnings from labor is on a par with forced labor."[2] Samuel Wheeler proposes an intriguing analogy in support of Nozick's position. "No significant moral difference in kind exists between eliminating my ability to play softball by taking my knees away and my ability to play the market by taking my money away," Wheeler writes. "Theft, taxation, and disembowelment are different forms of the same kind of violations of rights."[3] On the Nozick/Wheeler account, individuals own themselves (an ownership interest government must protect via criminal prohibitions of *WFF*), but no further coercive power may be exercised by the state.

The minimalist conception of justice might be challenged directly. That is, someone might insist, as a definitional matter, that justice necessarily includes obligations of support *as well as* obligations of restraint and so might contend that an advocate of minimalism misunderstands the nature of justice. The sections that follow take a different approach. They begin by showing that, contrary to the minimalist conception, it's widely assumed that the physically disabled are entitled, as a matter of justice, to social support that will provide them with fair equality of opportunity in their dealings with others. In doing so, the chapter lays the foundation for a general thesis about social justice, one that defends the legitimacy of government initiatives that redistribute wealth to ensure fair equality of opportunity for everyone born into a political community. The chapter then shows that even the minimalist conception of justice outlined earlier (i.e., the one limited to rights of self-ownership) can, at least under certain circumstances, yield a commitment to redistributive government initiatives that promote fair equality of opportunity. Finally, the chapter's last section returns to the premise noted at the outset—i.e., that a decent society is one that promotes social justice (understood as a commitment to redistributive initiatives that promote obligations of support) and *also* criminal justice (understood as a commitment to enforcement of core obligations of restraint). This conception of a decent society will serve as a criterion for assessing the legitimacy of modern initiatives involving *WFF*.

A Modest Challenge to the Minimalist Version of Justice: The Case of the Americans with Disabilities with Act

Consider first a relatively straightforward challenge to the minimalist version of justice. Although many people embrace the minimalist conception of justice as a matter of abstract principle (or at least something roughly similar), they also tend to accept the legitimacy of tax-supported intervention on behalf of those born with physical disabilities. The Americans with Disabilities Act, adopted in 1990 and amended on many subsequent occasions, underscores this point, for its provisions have secured majority support multiple times.[4] Pursuant to the act, people born with physical (and also cognitive) disabilities may invoke the government's power to increase the possibility of equalizing their life chances by comparison with those who are disability-free. The equalizing measures may be modest (extra time on a test, for instance), but they are sometimes substantial (installing elevators in subways). However extensive they are, though, their cost is *not* borne by the people benefiting from them. Rather, it's borne by the public at large. That is, people not disadvantaged by the circumstances of their birth pay (sometimes via taxes, sometimes via user fees) for initiatives designed to place the disabled on a roughly equal footing with those who are not. To put the point differently, the ADA aims at overcoming disadvantages occasioned by the birth lottery—not at overcoming them entirely, but at overcoming them to a significant degree (and thus at promoting fair equality of opportunity).

Is this framework unjust? Does it amount to a form of legalized extortion by requiring *A* (a person without disabilities) to subsidize *B* (a disabled person)? No definitive answer to this question is possible.

Someone who follows Nozick's statement that "taxation of earnings from labor is on a par with forced labor" can't be charged with incoherence for rejecting even the ADA's modest move beyond the minimalist conception of justice. Because *I* never agreed to support the disabled, a Nozick follower might argue, the government engages in unjust coercion in compelling me to equalize their life chances. There is no logical flaw in this assertion. No argument suggesting that minimalism is internally incoherent will be advanced in the pages that follow.

However, a different kind of argument—one that builds on the thought experiment employed in the previous chapter to justify the state's use of coercive force against even those who are unwilling to refrain from *WFF*—can, and will be, advanced here. In deploying this approach, someone endorses not merely obligations of restraint but, at a minimum, those obligations of support that aim at ensuring fair equality of opportunity. *I may not have been born with a disability*, the person adopting this approach says, *but because I might have been, I would reason in terms of a framework that makes government the enforcer of a collective insurance scheme, one in which people born with disabilities receive tax-generated subsidies that contribute to equalization of their life chances.*

The *would* in this sentence is critical, of course. An advocate of this more extensive conception of justice recognizes that the judgment of people born *without* disabilities may be clouded by their current condition—and so recognizes that a person ignorant of his/her circumstances (i.e., ignorant of his or her fate in the birth lottery) would agree to have government enforce a collective insurance scheme on behalf of the disabled even though people who *already* know that they are not disabled might not agree on this. In using this method (i.e., a thought experiment) to identify the fair terms of cooperation, we aim at banishing the distortive effect of someone's actual circumstances. Instead, we imagine what rationally self-interested individuals *ignorant of the actual circumstances of their birth* would expect of an enforcement agency charged with fulfilling the fair terms of cooperation.

A similar framework was used in the previous chapter. In adopting the non-ideal framework employed there, we concluded that someone aware of his/her specific circumstances (aware of his physical strength, for instance, or aware of her wealth and social connections) would be reluctant to agree to the establishment of a central enforcement agency for addressing acts of *WFF*, for those benefiting from the actual circumstances of their birth (the physically and socially advantaged, for instance) might well calculate that they would profit more from acts of aggression than they would from living under an agency charged with enforcing the obligations of restraint—and so might want to avoid being encumbered by an institution that prohibits acts of aggression.

The disabilities thought experiment outlined here builds on, but isn't identical to, the one used for criminal justice. That is, it builds on the earlier one by eliminating the distortive effect of personal circumstances on the exercise of judgment about the fair terms of cooperation. But it extends the conclusion concerning obligations of restraint by identifying obligations of support essential to the terms of communal life as a matter of ideal theory. In this respect, we've gone beyond the minimalist account of justice to suggest that the physically disabled have a right (a right that can properly be enforced via government's coercive power) to support in the form of material aid from those who are physically capable.

A More Comprehensive Version of Social Justice

The path to a more comprehensive version of social justice is now clear. In following it, we will continue to employ the thought experiment methodology already used, but we will now consider government interventions designed to correct disadvantages of birth associated with race, class, and gender. This is social justice as that term is used in everyday speech. As noted, even more ambitious versions of social justice can be imagined. That is, someone might assert that the fair terms of cooperation don't meet the standards of justice unless *outcomes* are roughly similar. This is *not* the version that will be defended here. Rather, we will adopt the following framework: we will assume that rationally self-interested people prepared to engage in cooperative activity with one another and unaware of their specific, individualizing characteristics would agree to establish a government that undertakes initiatives which correct for racial, class, and gender disadvantages associated with birth.

To use a phrase already introduced, this is the *fair equality of opportunity* version of social justice (FEO), now applied not merely to physical and cognitive disabilities but to disadvantages attributable to the general social structure.[5] Under FEO, *un*equal outcomes in social life are justified as long as government takes steps needed to promote roughly similar life chances for all its citizens. A framework such as this allows for the possibility that people will devote different amounts of effort to their work—and it thus allows for legitimate disparities in life outcomes through the operation of just social institutions.

The framework does *not*, however, allow for different degrees of government investment in each person's life. This is a point pertinent to race, class, *and* gender. As for the last category, FEO calls on government to adopt measures that equalize life chances in the face of the different biological functions of men and women. As for the first two, FEO calls on government not merely to take steps that prohibit discrimination but also to undertake proactive measures that correct for social and economic disadvantages attributable to the circumstances of birth. Each of these points is concerned with justice, not with charity. FEO is concerned, in other words, with a *right* to corrective measures regarding the circumstances of birth. It is not based on a *hope* for generosity on the part of the state or other any source of munificence. Instead, FEO is based on a commitment to systemic justice.

Why would a person who enjoys substantial advantages vis-a-vis other members of society agree to such a right? The answer to this is to be found in the conditional verb *would*. Experience has shown that the socially advantaged typically *do not* agree to measures that will compromise their position with regard to others. Some do, of course, but public policy is usually shaped by majority preferences, and the kind of equalizing measures just discussed are relatively rare (some of the most important exceptions, as noted, have to do with disabilities). Consideration of the thought experiment methodology demonstrates, however, why a comprehensive version of FEO is socially just—and why deliberators *would* agree to this if unaware of their individualizing characteristics. This is because it's reasonable to suppose that deliberators whose judgment is not distorted by the actual circumstances of their lives—i.e., deliberators who are uncertain whether they would benefit from, or be harmed by, arrangements that seek to equalize life chances—would adopt the initiatives essential to FEO. On this analysis, rational deliberators would avoid the *equal outcome* option, for they would consider it excessively intrusive to adopt a framework in which government might routinely revise property holdings to ensure equal results. And rational deliberators would also avoid the *minimalist* version of justice, for they would conclude that this framework exposes them to too much risk of disadvantage. Instead, they would conclude that FEO holds out the prospect of a genuinely just social order, one that treats government as the agency appropriate for implementing a collective insurance scheme that would still provide leeway for the exercise of individual initiative.

Readers acquainted with the philosophical literature pertinent to social justice will have recognized by now the degree to which the argument advanced here relies on the conclusions reached by, and the methodology essential to, John Rawls in *A Theory of Justice*. The conclusions aren't, however, wholly identical with those of Rawls, for among other things Rawls argues for a different principle concerning income distribution *as well as* FEO whereas the argument just considered focuses only on the latter possibility.[6] The methodology also differs in an important respect from that of Rawls. This is because Rawls does not employ it, as the previous chapter does, to introduce principles of criminal justice.[7] What's been proposed in this chapter and the preceding one, in other words, is a variation on Rawlsian thought, not a reiteration of it, a variation that suggests it may be possible to harmonize social justice and criminal justice—by employing non-ideal *and* ideal theory to identify the proper terms of communal life.

Revisiting the Minimalist Version of Justice

What if someone were to dissent from the arguments proposed so far on behalf of the obligations of support? In particular, what if someone were to say that the thought experiment methodology used here doesn't justify a firm conclusion as to the effects of the birth lottery, whether with respect to the physically disabled or people born into social disadvantage? A critic might claim, for instance, that the thought experiment outlined earlier in this chapter might not produce a conclusion in favor of taxpayer support for the disabled, for rational deliberators ignorant of their special circumstances might conclude that the risks of being born with a birth defect are so modest that they would choose not to be taxed to support people with such a condition. A similar point might be made about the conclusions rational deliberators would reach concerning other features of the birth lottery. The chances of being born into deprived circumstances are limited, this critic might say, and in any event the prospect of this is so substantially outweighed by the benefits of being born into wealth or of acquiring it by lawful means that social justice strategies favoring redistributive taxation would not be adopted *even* by rational deliberators unaware of their specific circumstances.

A critic taking this position would continue to agree that the thought experiment proposed in the first chapter provides a justification for the criminal justice thesis, for the critic would grant that, when anyone unaware of his/her specific circumstances calculates the possibility of being vulnerable to predation, the threat of *WFF* is sufficiently great as to make it essential to rely on a central enforcement agency. But the critic would refuse to go beyond this. Thought experiments in favor of even modest obligations of support are too speculative, too fraught with uncertainty, this critic might say, to warrant adoption of a framework that authorizes government to use its power to compel one person to support another. Better to call it quits at the criminal justice thesis, this critic would say, and to add to it one further feature: a principle that authorizes government to enforce the *voluntary* agreements people make when contracting with one another.

This, of course, is the minimalist conception of justice outlined earlier, one that's worth revisiting now that we've considered arguments for obligations of mutual support. What follows concedes the internal coherence of justice minimalism. It will be argued, though, that even minimalism mandates obligations of support once consideration is given to the history of government-initiated *WFF* and the accumulated social disadvantages this has brought about. Two steps should be followed to reach this (admittedly surprising) conclusion.

The first step is to note that minimalist justice requires a principle of compensation for acts of *WFF*. This corrective principle follows necessarily from the core tenets of non-ideal justice, for not only is punishment a possibility for predatory acts of *WFF*, compensation is required for the victims of these acts, particularly when government has perpetrated them. To reject this extension of minimalism would be to undermine the force of the voluntary contract principle, for a framework that supports acts of exchange is defensible only if people know that the choices they make won't be clouded by threats of *WFF*. Corrective measures for acts of *WFF* are thus an inescapable corollary of any framework of non-ideal justice, including the minimalist one. This point was made in the introduction when ideal and non-ideal theory were said to be complementary. We now see its relevance to justice minimalism.

The corrective justice principle just outlined is a common feature of legal systems as far as private parties are concerned. The principle applies to auto accidents and also to acts of fraud. If *A* damages *B*'s car, it holds, *A* must compensate *B*. Similarly, it holds that if *C* secures assets from *D* on the basis of a false representation, *C* must compensate *D*. The corrective justice principle embraces *WFF*, in other words. Put differently, *WFF* is a subject pertinent to compensatory *as well as* criminal justice.

The second step toward social justice through analysis of the ramifications of the minimalist conception applies the principles of corrective justice to government itself. In those settings where government has used its power to engage in acts of *WFF*, government is obligated to provide corrective justice, someone reasoning along these lines would contend. In particular, where government has used its power to benefit one segment of the population through brutal acts that deprive people of their personal liberty or property (i.e., wrongful force) or where government has made misrepresented its exercise of power (i.e., fraud), government must undertake corrective measures that address the cumulative disadvantages attributable to its acts. This second step is specific to certain societies. It's possible to imagine a society *without* a history of government-initiated wrongs that have benefited group *A* at the expense of group *B*, and for a society such as this the argument about to be advanced doesn't apply. However, all societies in the western hemisphere have such a history, as do many others as well, not only those in Australia and Africa but also those in Europe that engaged in colonialist exploitation of other portions of Eurasia and of South America, so the claims at stake here are pertinent to a great number of political communities.

Once this second step is taken, questions of social justice must be considered by advocates of the minimalist version of justice. They arise indirectly, of course. That is, although an advocate of the minimalist version rejects the conclusions reached above for providing *direct* government support on behalf of the disadvantaged, this advocate nonetheless must confront the weight of the corrective justice principle for providing *indirect* support, at least in societies with a history of conquest and exploitative subjugation.

It's well-known, of course, that government power was used throughout the western hemisphere and in many other parts of the world to dispossess aboriginal peoples and to enslave them and others. Government initiatives that dispossessed the aboriginal inhabitants of huge portions of the western hemisphere and Australia—sometimes through wrongful force, sometimes through fraud backed up by wrongful force—are standard features of the history of the last five hundred years. A parallel point applies to slavery, which also was enforced primarily by means of wrongful force employed by government agents, though sometimes by means of fraud. At stake here are massive, legally authorized acts of *WFF* that occurred in the distant past and that are thus distinguishable from acts of private-party wrongdoing in that they (a) involve politically approved *WFF* that (b) occurred a long time ago. (Needless to say, the issues Mandela addressed are pertinent in this context as well, though politically approved *WFF* occurred in South Africa's relatively recent past.)

It can't reasonably be argued that the fact that wrongdoing occurred on a massive scale or the further fact that it occurred in the distant past render issues of corrective justice irrelevant. On the contrary, massive state-sponsored wrongdoing makes corrective justice even more urgent than it is when, say, a fender-bender is at stake. Similarly, the fact that the wrongdoing was rarely addressed in the distant past also makes corrective justice more urgent than it would otherwise be, for this means that the disadvantages attributable to government wrongdoing have accumulated over time, compounding the loss people initially suffered. These vestiges of the past can't be shrugged off. Indeed, by treating prohibitions of *WFF* as the starting point for inquiry into justice, someone concentrates attention (though perhaps unwittingly) on the question of how to redress the vestiges of the past.

How should redress be provided? One possible answer is to apply the fender-bender model on a giant scale. Under that model, someone seeks to undo harm—i.e., the person adopting this model aims at restoring the victim to the condition he/she would have occupied but for the wrong. An inquiry of this kind requires consideration of counterfactual issues: what was the victim's condition before the wrong occurred, what is the victim's condition now, and what would the victim's condition be had the wrong not occurred? We can call this a *tracing inquiry*. In undertaking it we hazard a guess that's essential to undoing a wrong. An inquiry of this kind requires resolution of speculative issues. It has to be granted that speculation is always hazardous. Nonetheless, once allowance is made for the uncertainties associated with its counterfactual questions, one might defend it as a principled way to implement the core features of corrective justice.

It's sometimes contended that a similar approach should be applied to the vestiges of historic wrongs. In furthering this idea, the term *reparations* is often used to refer to the compensation due descendants of historic wrongs for the accumulated disadvantages they have suffered.[8]

The attraction of a reparations framework is that it relies, as does the fender-bender model, on a one-and-done solution to corrective justice issues—that is, victims receive a lump-sum payment (perhaps stretched over many years, but a lump-sum in that the amount paid is computed at a single moment in time) for the entire amount due them for the harm they've suffered. Some features of the lump-sum approach are surely desirable, for when it's used people can operate on the assumption that the problems of the past have been fully, and satisfactorily, addressed.

There are, however, substantial difficulties with this approach—and these outweigh its merits. One difficulty has to do with tracing, for once historical changes in migration and intermarriage are considered, it becomes nearly impossible to connect those currently alive with those wronged in the distant past. A further difficulty has to do with the degree of harm suffered in the past, for the historical record makes it impossible to reach a sound conclusion about how much harm was inflicted and how it impacted later generations. And third, the very notion of *undoing* seems inappropriate here. What would this mean as far as indigenous people are concerned? Giving back land that was taken by force and fraud? Calculating the increased market value of that land by comparison with its value at the time of its wrongful acquisition and then paying damages by reference to this increase? And what it would mean for the descendants of African-American slaves? Calculating the value of their ancestors' enforced labor? Imposing a special surcharge on the descendants of the sailors who piloted slave ships?

Given these problems, it's best to grant, on the one hand, that the vestiges of the past are inescapable (i.e., to agree that those who are most disadvantaged today are disproportionately descendants of those who were disadvantaged by massive historic wrongs) but also to grant that there is no reasonable way to identify, on a person-for-person basis, the exact monetary burden the past has imposed on the present. In light of these points, we should set aside the possibility of a lump-sum payment and instead adopt the social justice framework outlined earlier. As noted before, this is a society-specific conclusion, one that doesn't apply universally but only to those societies with a history of massive wrongs. We needn't consider this point further here, for it's manifestly relevant to every country in the western hemisphere and to many in other regions of the globe—relevant, in other words, on such a large scale as to warrant discussion under the general heading *social justice*.

Rather than comment further on the merits of this approach, it would be helpful to turn to remarks by Robert Nozick, a leading proponent of the minimalist approach to justice, that point toward the same conclusion concerning obligations of support. As an advocate of justice minimalism, Nozick espouses the principle of self-ownership, and he thus advocates limiting government power to prohibitions of *WFF* plus enforcement of contracts. In particular, Nozick argues in *Anarchy, State, and Utopia*, a key tract in modern libertarianism, that the type of thought experiment outlined in the previous section of this chapter doesn't provide a conclusive justification for taxing *A* to correct for the disadvantageous circumstances of *B*'s birth.[9] But Nozick doesn't stop there; he also grants that the minimalist version of justice must be supplemented by a corrective justice principle (he calls it a *rectification principle*) that addresses not only modest private-party wrongs (fender-benders and the like) but also massive societal wrongs. He does so in a passage that's worth careful consideration since it underscores the importance of compensating victims acts of state-sponsored injustice (even descendants of these victims) through reliance on a framework of justice that otherwise rejects the legitimacy of the concept of obligations outlined in the previous sub-section.

If the state undertakes initiatives based on *WFF*, Nozick writes, "the principle of rectification comes into play." A response to these violations of *WFF*, he states, should include.

> some patterned principles of distributive justice as rough rules of thumb meant to approximate the general results of applying the principle of rectification of injustice. For example, lacking much historical information, and assuming (1) that victims of injustice generally do worse than they otherwise would and (2) that those from the least well-off group in the society have the highest probabilities of being the (descendants of) victims of the most serious injustice who are owed compensation by those who benefited from the injustices, ... then a *rough* rule of thumb for rectifying injustices might seem to be the following: organize society so as to maximize the position of whatever group ends up least well-off in society.[10]

In a society with a history of unaddressed historic wrongs, in other words, corrective justice calls for an ongoing program of wealth redistribution to benefit descendants of victims of those wrongs (provided, of course, the tracing problems at stake are so severe that it's impossible to connect each person currently alive with their wronged forbears). Advocates of the minimal version of justice tend to disregard this corollary to their commitments. The corollary is inescapable, though, once someone grants that the state's function isn't simply to prohibit *WFF* but also to refrain from *WFF* itself. This point having been granted, a prohibition on *WFF* calls not only for a central enforcement agency that punishes acts of predation, it also calls for redistributive measures that benefit descendants of the victims of that agency's own acts of predation.

Convergence and Complementarity

Although their starting points are different, the two approaches to justice examined in this chapter converge on a straightforward conclusion, one that assigns the state a critical role in enforcing mutual obligations of support in a way that aids the most disadvantaged members of society. On a minimalist account of justice, this conclusion is historically contingent: it holds only for countries with a history of systematic violations of rights of self-ownership. On the alternative account based on the thought experiment methodology outlined earlier, the requisites of social justice apply across the board. Important as this difference is, it isn't critical as far as the United States and many other developed countries are concerned. This is because the United States, all other countries in the Western hemisphere, and many countries in other parts of the world have a heritage of massive, state-sponsored historic wrongs. We can thus speak of a general requirement for government to enforce obligations of support that promote fair equality of opportunity. For these communities, social justice isn't a luxury item produced by the feverish brain. Rather, it's something that's due every member of the political community.

Given these points, we can say that there's a complementary relationship between criminal justice and social justice. As noted in the previous chapter, the criminal law operates in a way that has the potential to compromise justice, for it's administered by acts of domination carried out by agents of the state. In contrast, social justice aims at freeing people from market-based domination. The two kinds of justice, it thus might be said, are in tension with one another. On close inspection, though, it can be seen that they are mutually reinforcing, for when the domination essential to the operation of state-imposed coercion is limited to acts of

WFF and is conducted according to fair procedures, this sustains cooperation within the public sphere—and so promotes the possibility of social justice.

The next chapter examines the way in which the framework of domination essential to criminal law can be abused to further social injustice. These two chapters have established the reverse, however. They have shown that the limited type of domination effectuated by a just system of criminal law can sustain a cooperative social order. Obligations of restraint and obligations of support are components of a decent society, for the possibility of being held accountable for wrongful acts serves as an incentive to engage in mutually beneficial activity that each person has a roughly equal chance of engaging in. This point will inform discussion in the next section as we turn to alternative ways of approaching the social justice/criminal justice connection.

Notes

1. As quoted in David Cecil, *The Young Melbourne & Lord M* 233 [1949 and 1954] (2017).
2. Robert Nozick, *Anarchy, State, and Utopia* 169 (1974).
3. Samuel Wheeler, "Natural Property Rights as Body Rights," *Nous* 14: 171, 186 (1980).
4. Americans with Disabilities Act (ADA), 42 U.S.C. Sections 12,100 et seq. The ADA has been supplemented by the Individuals with Disabilities Act, 20 U.S.C. 2000 et seq.
5. The discussion of fair equality of opportunity in this paragraph is strongly indebted to Rawls's analysis of the term. See Rawls, *supra* note 3 in Introduction, 73–78. The limited Rawlsian version of social justice discussed here amounts to a particularly cautious conception of the idea. For a robust, luck egalitarian version, see Elizabeth Anderson, "What Is the Point of Equality?" *Ethics* 109: 287 (1999).
6. See Rawls, *supra* note 3 in Introduction, 65–73.
7. Rawls discusses criminal law, see id. at 276, but he does not discuss the concept of criminal justice. In any event, because Rawls's focus is on full compliance with the principles of justice (with what he calls "ideal theory," see id. 8), he does not investigate questions that, as he puts it, "weigh[] one form of institutional injustice

against another." (id.) This, of course, is an issue investigated at length in the chapters that follow.

8. For work on reparations that pursues these issues, see Dinah Shelton, "Reparations for Indigenous Peoples: The Present Value of Past Wrongs," in Federico Lenzerini, ed., *Reparations for Indigenous Peoples: International and Comparative Perspectives* (2008) 47–72; and William Darity, and Kristen Mullen, *From Here to Equality: Reparations and Black Americans in the Twenty-First Century* (2d ed., 2022).
9. For Nozick's critique of Rawls, see Nozick, *supra* note 2, at 150–228.
10. Id. 230–31. Because Nozick's first two principles of justice (the principle of acquisition of holdings and the principle of transfer of holdings) identify what he calls the necessary conditions of what he calls a "wholly just" society (id. 151), he can be said to reason in terms of ideal theory in developing them. But because Nozick adds a third principle to his first two, one that mandates rectification of acts that violate the earlier principles, he can also be said to reason in terms of non-ideal theory, a subject Rawls declines to address. In this respect, Nozick proposes a more comprehensive theory of justice than does Rawls, one that not only identifies the terms of communal life in an ideal society but that also considers the steps that should be taken for addressing historically significant violations of those terms. The remaining chapters of this book fuse ideal and non-ideal theory, though from a perspective that is not Nozick's.

PART II

Social Justice/Criminal Justice

CHAPTER 3

Dystopian Possibilities

Having examined the principles of criminal and social justice in isolation from one another, we're now in a position to consider the relationship between the two types of justice. This chapter examines a negative connection: ***dystopian possibilities***: the way in which injustice in society at large is reproduced through administration of criminal law. The next chapter, entitled ***utopian possibilities***, considers something quite different: the prospect of dispensing entirely with criminal law on achieving a full measure of social justice.

Nelson Mandela's remarks on South Africa introduced us to an unmistakably dystopian possibility, one involving political, not social, injustice. Mandela didn't engage in the kind of behavior typically prohibited by a penal code. He didn't resort to wrongful force or fraud: his advocacy was non-violent and it was certainly not fraudulent, so it can't be said that his criminal conviction in 1963 conforms to the model followed adopted by, say, the Jim Crow south. This said, his conviction is nonetheless an example of social injustice/criminal injustice in a larger sense of the term, for apartheid's aim—its rationale—was to perpetuate an unjust racial hierarchy.

Moreover, once we reason in terms of this capacious version of social injustice, we can readily agree that Mandela's conviction is an easy case—not easy in the sense that it's morally acceptable (on the contrary, it's a paradigm case of injustice). Rather, it's easy in the sense that no serious

W. C. Heffernan, *Social Justice/Criminal Justice*,
https://doi.org/10.1007/978-3-031-75397-8_3

investigation of the principles of criminal and social justice is needed to establish the wrongfulness of his sentence. This chapter investigates other cases, some also easy, but harder ones as well. It does so in three sections. The first examines straightforward examples of government use of power to sustain a legally sanctioned system of social injustice. The connecting link for the examples used in the first section is that, like Mandela's 1963 case, they're drawn from the past. They're thus subject to effortless rebuke from the present, for no substantial price is paid when someone holds up defunct practices for criticism as morally unacceptable. Nonetheless, it's valuable now to identify what was wrong then, for in doing so someone can treat the past as offering a cautionary lesson for what's to be avoided today.

The chapter's second section addresses cautionary lessons drawn from the present. It considers two arguments that suggest the past has been replicated in the current legal and social system—and arguments that further suggest it is *systemically* replicated in contemporary practice, with the result that the prospects for legal change are minimal to nonexistent unless the social system is modified substantially. This is dystopian reasoning about criminal justice in the context of social justice. It holds that, no matter how fair the legal procedures followed in convicting someone of a crime (no matter how even-handed police practices may be when investigating a suspect's criminality, no matter how zealously a defense lawyer defends his/her client, no matter how impartial jurors may be), criminal conviction of a defendant who hasn't received the requisites of social justice is, at a minimum, tainted and, perhaps, wholly unjust. In evaluating this argument, the second section concludes that, as long as a contemporary jurisdiction limits its coercive power to conducting impartial, even-handed inquiry into acts of *WFF*, conviction can't be rejected as morally illegitimate, though it may often be tainted. The book's final chapters (five through ten) consider steps that should be taken to reduce the taint.

The chapter's final section summarizes the complex arguments and policy premises it has presented. In analyzing the history of social injustice through criminal injustice, it makes the following points. The first is that contemporary critics are right to emphasize that vestiges of a socially unjust past continue to affect operation of the operation of the legal system. The second is that this makes it imperative to limit the scope of state penal power, in particular to focus on individual accountability and to de-emphasize punishment. But third, the chapter contends that the state continues to play an indispensable role as the accountability-seeking institution of communal life, for even though the state's earlier role in promoting social injustice is indisputable, there is still no other organization—nor is there a prospect of one—that can adopt impartial procedures that call on people to account for the harm they've brought about. This is merely a summary of the arguments that will be considered concerning dystopian possibilities. A further concluding summary will be included in the next chapter, which is concerned with utopian possibilities. After that, we will turn to steps, neither dystopian nor utopian, that can inject social justice considerations into the operation of the criminal law.

State Capture: Examples from the Past

The term *state capture* was introduced by economists in the early 2000s as they examined the way in which corrupt groups took control of the apparatus of power in post-communist regimes.[1] Since then, the term has been employed more broadly. It is now used by political scientists as well as economists to focus on the way in which elites have leveraged their legislative power within a community to secure legally sanctioned monopolies for themselves.[2] This sub-section expands further on the term. It uses *state capture* to examine the way one faction within a political community exercises control over that community's legal system to ensure the subjugation of another faction. The political community under consideration may be a nation-state; eighteenth-century England will be used to think about this. Alternatively, the political community may be a state within a nation-state; early twentieth states in the American south will be used to illustrate this kind of state capture by means of Jim Crow.

Consider eighteenth-century England first. As a result of the revolution of 1688, English aristocrats amassed decisive power for themselves: they drove one king (James II) off the throne; they selected his replacements (William and Mary); and they enjoyed supermajority control of both Houses of Parliament. Throughout the eighteenth century, this elite, known as the Whig oligarchs, sponsored legislation that furthered their domestic economic interests and adopted policies that expanded English expansion throughout the world.[3] Even before the eighteenth century, aristocrats had played a decisive role, by serving as justices of the peace, in administering the criminal law.[4] With the Black Acts, first adopted in 1723 and renewed on subsequent occasions in slightly different form, the Whig oligarchs used their dominant legislative position to tighten their hold on the country's lower classes. Under the Black Acts (so-called because trespassers blackened their faces while venturing onto estates in search of deer and other game), someone found guilty of trespass while stealing food was liable to execution. Though applicable to anyone, the class ramifications of the statute were nonetheless obvious, for the poor rather than the rich are of course likeliest to trespass on private property in search of food. An economic elite had deployed the state's monopoly of legitimate power, in other words, to ensure the subjugation of the poor.[5]

Though ominous in principle, the Black Acts proved to be less than entirely effective in practice. Prosecutions under it were brought, and trespassers were occasionally put to death. But the ultimate penalty was only sometimes sought, and juries often recoiled at the prospect of conviction given the possibility of execution. The Black Acts functioned more as *in terrorem* measures designed to keep the poor in their place, then, and not as an actual measure of inhumane legal control.[6] Even when viewed in light of this pattern of sporadic enforcement, though, the Black Acts nonetheless serve as a telling example of class-based state capture, for they functioned as protective measures that shielded wealth at the expense of the basic needs of the vast majority of the population.

In the case of the Jim Crow south, state capture had two complementary functions. On the one hand, peonage preserved the economic subordination of Blacks even after the Thirteenth Amendment brought slavery to an end. On the other hand, Jim Crow legislation sustained a political structure in which planters dominated poorer Whites (though the latter were enfranchised), and Whites of all classes dominated Blacks (who were disenfranchised).[7]

The Jim Crow statutes that imposed legally mandated segregation emerged only gradually in the quarter century following the end of Reconstruction in 1877. There is an important sense in which statutes to this effect weren't needed in the South following the legal demise of slavery, for even before adoption of the Thirteenth Amendment contact between Blacks and Whites was based on a code of behavior that reinforced the inferior social, political, and economic status of the former vis a vis the latter. During the first decades of the twentieth century, though, the planter elite exploited their dominant position in state legislatures by adopting statutes and codes that regulated voting, education, and access to public transportation and other facilities. The Supreme Court upheld the constitutionality of Jim Crow's "separate but equal" legislative framework in *Plessy v. Ferguson*, an 1896 case.[8] The Court subsequently affirmed *Plessy's* framework in numerous other cases decided in the first third of the twentieth century.[9]

Plessy was concerned with explicit racial classifications. In contrast, criminal law in the Jim Crow south operated not by means of racial categories contained in legislation but by means of prosecutorial discretion that favored Whites over Blacks. Though distinguishable for this reason from the racially explicit laws that governed matters such as education and public transportation, Jim Crow criminal law was an indispensable component of the entire southern social structure, for it was by terrorizing Blacks that state capture could be perpetuated. Framing innocent defendants was one component of legalized terror. Not surprisingly, no data can be found as to the frequency of framing Black defendants. It seems likely, though, that there were many more instances of framing than the few cases in which it can now be established that this occurred, for it was only when criminal defense lawyers could produce reliable evidence to challenge the state's claims of guilt that a clear-cut argument for framing could be made. The Scottsboro cases of the early 1930s serve as a straightforward example of prosecutorial framing. Even after one of the White complaining witnesses in the cases admitted that she had lied about being raped, prosecutors persisted in seeking the death penalty for the Black defendants who had been charged—and so revealed the *in terrorem* premise essential to Jim Crow administration of the criminal law.[10]

Framing defendants may have been rare. When we turn to data about inter- and intraracial homicides, a subject about which the figures are relatively reliable, we can see how routinely prosecutorial discretion was employed to perpetuate the social structure of racial subordination. Homicide statistics compiled by Hortense Powdermaker in her 1939 study of Indianola, a town in the Mississippi delta, underscore the critical role played by prosecutorial discretion in sustaining the Jim Crow criminal law. White-on-White killings were almost always prosecuted, though they didn't always result in the death penalty, Powdermaker reported. Black killings of whites always led to death, either by execution or lynching. White-on-Black killings were almost never prosecuted; as Powdermaker remarked, "[w]hen a white man kills a Negro, it is hardly considered murder." Black-on-Black homicides also weren't taken seriously; only about 30% of these appear to have been prosecuted.[11]

Each of these patterns merits special attention. Prosecutors responded to White-on-White homicide in roughly the way one would expect given the criminal justice thesis outlined in the first chapter. Today, their response would perhaps be rejected by contemporary commentators as too severe, but the insistence on holding offenders to account for their violations of the obligations of restraint can certainly be deemed proper. Prosecutors' response to Black-on-White murders is understandable in terms of the criminal law's function of ensuring Black subordination. This is the best-known feature of Jim Crow criminal law. It is understandable not in terms of *non*-accountability—in terms of the state's failure to enforce the obligations of restraint.

Important as this point is, it has to be considered in light of something equally significant but less frequently noted—i.e., the relaxation (to the point of nearly complete indifference to) of legal accountability as far as Black-on-Black homicides are concerned. Just as Jim Crow resulted in draconian sentences (when lynching didn't occur) for Black-on-White murder, it resulted in *under*enforcement of the law in murders with Black victims. Accountability was routinely *not* sought in this instance, in other words. The state's monopoly power was used to sustain a social structure organized around the morally arbitrary features of each person's birth.

Political Capture: Examples from the Present

How much has changed? As is well known, in 1954, *Brown v. Board of Education* overruled *Plessy v. Ferguson*, thereby leading to dismantlement of the regime of racial segregation in public places.[12] Moreover, the Jim Crow stranglehold over the political process was profoundly disrupted when the Voting Rights Act of 1965 was adopted.[13] As a result of these changes, Blacks participated in education and public life as they never had before. In particular, Black membership in legislatures began to expand, and Blacks began to staff and administer the legal system. Moreover, government spending on behalf of the poor increased dramatically at the same time. Medicare and Medicaid were created; college enrollments expanded; *Gideon v. Wainwright* guaranteed legal representation for indigent defendants. On one way of thinking about these trends, state capture gave way to a condition approaching social justice. In particular, someone advancing a triumphalist argument along these lines might contend that a new political order was established that made it possible for previously excluded segments of the public to pursue power in the legislative arena—and even to capture it on some issues—and thus to participate in the creation of a legal framework free of class oppression and the racial animus of the past.

Many commentators treat the changes just discussed as evidence of profound change. Others, in contrast, emphasize the persistence of vestiges of the past, particularly when thinking about class and race in the administration of criminal law. Loic Wacquant, whose *Punishing the Poor: The Neoliberal Government of Social Insecurity* was published in 2009, emphasizes the degree to which criminal law perpetuates class domination. On Wacquant's account, the modern state imposes punishment only incidentally as a response to wrongdoing and primarily to preserve the subordinate position of those who are already disadvantaged. The "'new penology' being put in place does not aim at 'rehabilitating' criminals," Wacquant argues; rather, it aims at "managing costs and controlling dangerous populations."[14] Criminal punishment "warehouses" the poor, he asserts, "bend[ing] the fractions of the working-class recalcitrant to the discipline of the new fragmented service wage-labor into the informal economy of the street…."[15]

On this analysis, state-imposed punishment has only a tenuous connection to the criminal justice thesis outlined in the first chapter. Rather, it's understandable in terms of the state's unwillingness to undertake the kind of systemic change essential to the social justice initiatives outlined in the second chapter. It's understandable instead in terms of the cosmetic changes just mentioned (Medicare and Medicaid, expanded educational opportunities, and *Gideon* are hardly sufficient to equalize life chances for the truly disadvantaged)—while the criminal law continues to be deployed to manage an unruly underclass composed of expendable cogs in the ever-expanding service sector of the economy.

What reforms does Wacquant propose to mitigate the effects of the criminal law? To ask this question is to reveal a misunderstanding of the inquiry he's undertaking. His aim is to identify the characteristics of a system in which punishment of the poor functions as a way of perpetuating their subordinate social status. He doesn't argue that punishment is intentionally imposed for this purpose; he does, however, imply that the function is permanent—or at least that state-imposed punishment (the effect of which is to trap the underclass in a cycle of poverty and recurrent run-ins with the law) is likely for the indefinite future as long neoliberalism crowds out initiatives that fail to address the material needs of the underclass. Put differently, on Wacquant's analysis, the 1960s were insufficient. Systemic change is essential—and unlikely.

Michelle Alexander, author of *The New Jim Crow: Mass Incarceration in the Age of Colorblindness*, published in 2010, takes a similar approach, though her focus is on criminal law's effect on Blacks rather than its effect on the poor. "Everything has changed," she writes. "Yet nothing has. The politics of white supremacy, which defined our original constitution, have continued unabated—repeatedly and predictably engendering new systems of racial and social control."[16]

As with Wacquant, this seems to point toward an all-or-nothing approach to altering the criminal law: either everything changes beyond the administration of criminal law (Wacquant: dismantle the neoliberal service economy and replace it with a humane system of income redistribution; Alexander: end systemic racism by making members of ethnic minorities into full participants in the social order) or else nothing significant will change as far as legal outcomes are concerned. On this reckoning, social justice takes full precedence over criminal justice: as long as there is social injustice beyond the law, this will undermine administration within it. Cosmetic procedural changes (pertaining to search and seizure, bail, sentencing, etc.) may be undertaken, but these shouldn't distract us from the underlying structural reality.

Or at least this all-or-nothing reasoning appears to inform the approach taken by both Wacquant and Alexander. As it happens, Alexander has endorsed a reform that could modify the administration of criminal law without requiring the complete overhaul of the world beyond the law—a "something," to add a term to missing from the Alexander lexicon, that lies between "everything" and "nothing." The reform involves restorative justice, a process in which an offender is called on to account to his/her victim for harm caused, come to terms with the scope of this harm by listening to the victim's narrative, reconcile with the victim by taking responsibility for what he/she did, and then accept the victim's determination of the appropriate response (punishment, perhaps, but as Alexander points out, often community service or service to the victim accompanied by reconciliation). The restorative justice process is already widely used for minor crimes (for spray-painting the exterior of a victim's home or petit larceny, for example). What sets Alexander's proposal apart is that she advocates restorative justice for violent crimes (up to, and including, aggravated assault, rape, and murder).[17]

Here, then, is a genuine "something," a measure that might be adopted by legal authorities *without* altering the entire social system. In particular, it stands out for treating the process of holding someone accountable for harm as the bare-bones minimum for the administration of criminal law. That process necessarily draws on the state—on the state's deployment of its coercive power, it should be emphasized (for some people accused of harming others are unwilling to account for what they've done). This point is noted in the first chapter. Moreover, the first chapter advocates, as does Alexander, an accountability process without advancing a rationale for punishment—or to put the point somewhat differently, Alexander is agnostic, as is the first chapter, about specific justifications for punishment (retributive and incapacitative, for instance), though she necessarily endorses what most offenders might view as a deterrence rationale for the state's response to a victim's complaint (for the very fact that coercion is used in calling on a suspected offender to respond to an allegation of wrongdoing will have a general deterrent effect on those considering aggression against others).

In this respect, Alexander's accountability proposal is similar to the one that will be advocated throughout the remainder of the book. Each is bare-bones; each calls on the state to require answers to victim complaints; each deprecates punishment, however; and each treats incarceration as a last resort, rather than a preferred, option in responding to wrongdoing.

The Alexander proposal may differ in one important respect, however, for the criminal justice thesis outlined earlier (in this book's first chapter) vests final authority in state officials to dispose of a case—a jury, perhaps, or a judge—whereas Alexander appears to vest this in the victim. *Appears to* is essential here, for Alexander writes that on her version of restorative justice "survivors help to devise an accountability plan,"[18] with *help* leaving it unclear what party determines, in the end, how to dispose of the case. The accountability passages in the first chapter are clear on this point: state officials must have the final say, for they alone can ensure the degree of uniformity associated with the maxim *treat like cases alike*.

To this, we can add a corollary, not mentioned in the first chapter, a corollary that perhaps would be unacceptable to Alexander: not only is an accountability process necessary to set criminal law in motion (not a criminal trial, of course, a referral from a criminal court will suffice), but the disposition of a case must be subject to evaluation according to a culpability scale (not necessarily an inflexible one but, at least, a scale that presumptively ranks murder as more serious than rape and rape as more serious than aggravated assault, etc.). Such a scale shouldn't be confused with a sentencing grid. Without one, however, (and Alexander makes no reference either to a scale or to the importance of outcome-uniformity) fidelity to a victim's wishes might mean that one murder, fundamentally similar to another as far as fact-patterns are concerned, would lead to a vastly different disposition than another—or that the disposition of a rape would be more severe than the disposition of a murder. Even these outcomes might be acceptable given a culpability scale, for the scale should be formulated in presumptive terms. The presumptions should be rebuttable, however; seat-of-the-pants intuition shouldn't be the exclusive order of the day—and this, unfortunately, is the impression Alexander gives in outlining her restorative justice proposal.

One other byproduct of an emphasis on accountability merits attention. In focusing on personal accountability, an advocate of this approach tends to discount the significance of claims that treat an offender's history of social injustice as a mitigating factor that justifies a less severe sentence. By parity of reasoning, those reasoning in terms of personal accountability tend to discount a related, but clearly distinguishable, argument—that when the state has failed to provide an offender with the full requisites of social justice, it is unfit (unfit as a matter of political morality) to condemn that offender. Because Alexander focuses so intently on the social justice/criminal justice connection, it's somewhat surprising she doesn't address either issue. We should do so here, however, and should do so by setting aside mitigation claims based on the state's failure to provide the requisites of social justice (while nonetheless casting a skeptical eye on punishment).

As far as claims of mitigation are concerned, it seems unlikely that a sentencer can make an informed judgment about the degree of social justice deprivation an offender has suffered and the extent to which such a deprivation has interfered with the offender's capacity to conform to the law. Must the deprivation be profound, or will a modest one suffice? Should the offender's reaction matter—will "acting out" in response to a deprivation count as a reason for mitigation whereas internalization (i.e., blaming oneself) won't? Should an offender's sex matter (males are more likely to offend, and indeed male genes, particularly those of adolescent males, may be better predictors of a propensity to offend than most variables on offer)? Questions such as these underscore the uncertainties—and thus the potential for arbitrariness—in resolving mitigation claims based on social justice deprivations. Alexander takes the better approach by deprecating punishment and incarceration generally, but by otherwise sidestepping individualized claims of mitigation. Thus, although the objection to claims of mitigation advanced here may differ from Alexander's, they too avoid the perils of individualized determinations of eligibility for mitigation on the grounds of a social justice deprivation.

What about an alternative, then? What if someone were to argue that when government has failed to provide a defendant with the requisites of social justice, a further injustice—an impermissible one, it could be argued—occurs if the defendant is punished? This "dirty hands" argument (*government is unfit to impose punishment until it addresses its own injustices*) is analytically distinct from the mitigation claim examined above. It's best addressed by returning to a distinction between pathological and problematic systems of criminal law. Under Jim Crow (to use our paradigm, but by no means our only possible, example), the salient characteristic of a pathological legal system is to preserve status hierarchy, so the disposition of any case involving an allegation of interracial crime or of intraracial Black on Black crime must be classified on an across-the-board basis as not merely tainted but presumptively illegitimate.

Needless to say, this is merely a notional judgment: the elites that controlled the Jim Crow south were indifferent to criticism by the rest of the country—and of course are immune to it today. Nonetheless, this judgment of the past is instructive today: it sets the standard for evaluating the present. But has the past been replicated in the present? Is condemnation in order for a problematic, as distinguished from a pathological, legal system? In particular, is it in order for a system that is trying, albeit with less than complete success, to come to terms with its past?

The answer to this is by no means clear. Even today, the administration of criminal law continues to sustain social injustice. This point can't be considered in isolation from others, though. It's essential to ask what other institution might oversee the process of calling on suspects to account for their conduct. The answer is that alternatives to the state—an aggrieved family, for instance, or a neighborhood association—are likely to be less impartial than the state. Moreover, it certainly seems reasonable to say that a legal system whose officials are trying to overcome its past shortcomings while remaining committed to the rule of law should be endorsed, absent an obvious alternative, as the institution that oversees the accountability process that sets criminal justice in motion. Alexander appears to have taken this position—thus her approving comments on restorative justice as undertaken subject to the current legal system (for, after all, she comments skeptically on current law *but nonetheless advocates a restorative justice overseen by officials of the contemporary system*). In any event, this is the line of inquiry that will be pursued in the remainder of the book, for we will consider a much less punitive version of criminal justice in the pages that follow—but a version that's recognizably rooted in criminal justice since coercive state authority is exercised in calling on suspects to account for their conduct—in the course of integrating social justice considerations into the administration of criminal law. On this reckoning, the conclusions reached by the current legal system can properly be classified as tainted (and efforts should be made to eliminate the taint), but they shouldn't be rejected as illegitimate.

Setting Aside All-or-Nothing Binaries

If we step back, we can retrace the argument advanced here about dystopian versions of the social justice/criminal justice connection. The introduction to the book notes Mandela's claim that the criminal law of the Union of South Africa sustained that country's system of social injustice. This chapter has considered examples of the same phenomenon: (examples from earlier centuries of other legal systems that have furthered systemic social injustice). And contemporary critics have emphasized the continuity between past and present—that is, they've argued that vestiges of the past continue to be reinforced by today's criminal law. Contemporary criminal law may be procedurally sound (criminal defense lawyers may aggressively assert their clients' rights; judges may honor rules already laid down; juries may reach honest verdicts), but as long as the social order remains systemically unjust, these critics contend, that injustice will be reproduced by the legal system.

On this version of the systemic injustice thesis, issues of social justice take priority over criminal justice. In adopting this far-reaching version of the thesis, someone relies on an all-or-nothing binary, one in which injustice beyond the law must be modified before changes internal to the administration of criminal law provide relief for those charged with crimes. Wacquant appears to endorse this thesis. Alexander also appears to endorse it, given the continuity she emphasizes by entitling her book the *new* Jim Crow.

As we've seen, though, Alexander sets aside all-or-nothing binaries by proposing an internal legal reform (use of restorative justice to hold offenders accountable for their acts) that might be adopted *without* engaging in overhaul of the social structure. As we've also seen, a commitment to holding people accountable serves as a starting point for injecting social justice considerations into the operation of criminal law. Using state power to require accused offenders to account for their acts amounts to government-initiated coercion. Coercion in this context also has a deterrent effect, for few people welcome the prospect of answering for the harm they've brought about. Starting with personal accountability amounts to the "something" (the measure that sidesteps all-or-nothing reasoning) that lies between Alexander's "everything" and "nothing."

Calling on suspects to account for the harm they're charged with having caused will also be the informing premise for the proposals advocated in the remainder of the book. The accountability focus adopted here will differ in important respects from Alexander's approach. Among others, it will be accompanied by a culpability scale for ranking violent crimes. Moreover, the argument that will be advanced later will address the *Miranda* ramifications of uncounseled confessions and also the pertinence of psychiatric conclusions concerning undiagnosed disorders when suspects take personal responsibility for their acts. These points and others—points Alexander doesn't discuss—will qualify the emphasis on accountability. Once these qualifications are noted, though, it's essential to emphasize that a focus on accountability runs throughout the book, for (as Alexander also realizes) an argument that the criminal process begins with a hearing about accountability does not, by itself, lead to adoption of the premise that punishment must be imposed for harm done—and, in particular, this entails no commitment to incarceration. Requiring accused wrongdoers to respond to their accusers in a forum where their answers are evaluated by third-party observers meets the minimum standard set by the criminal justice thesis proposed in Chapter 1. It promotes the impartial administration of law. It's compatible with a limitation of the criminal sanction to acts of *WFF*. At the same time, it leaves considerable leeway for the integration of social justice considerations into the administration of criminal law.

Before turning to this way of rethinking criminal justice, we should consider a different perspective—one that focuses on the utopian possibility that full realization of social justice will make criminal law unnecessary—that's also relevant to the social justice/criminal justice connection. Because the chapters contained in Section III treat the current legal system as problematic rather than pathological in the road to improvement on the past, it's also essential to examine claims about the possibility of dispensing with criminal law entirely.

Notes

1. See, e.g., World Bank, *Anticorruption in Transition: A Contribution to the Policy Debate* (2000).
2. See, e.g., John Crabtree and Francisco Durand, *Peru: Elite Power and Political Capture* (2017).
3. For an overview, see Geoffrey Holmes and Daniel Szechi, *The Age of Oligarchy: Pre-Industrial Britain, 1722–1783* (1993).
4. For discussion of the role of justices of the peace in early modern England, see Hereward Senior, *Constabulary: The Rise of Police Institutions in Britain, the Commonwealth, and the United States* (1997).
5. See E.P. Thompson, *Whigs and Hunters: The Origin of the Black Act* (1975).
6. For discussion of the Black Act's enforcement, see John Langbein, "Albion's Fatal Flaws," *Past and Present* 98: 96 (1982).
7. See generally Michael Klarman, *From Jim Crow to Civil Rights: The Supreme Court and the Struggle for Racial Equality* Chap. 1 (2004).
8. *Plessy v. Ferguson*, 163 U.S. 537 (1896).
9. For an overview, see C. Vann Woodward, *The Strange Career of Jim Crow* (1955).
10. For discussion of the Scottsboro cases, see James Goodman, *Scottsboro Stories* (1995).
11. Hortense Powdermaker, *After Freedom: A Cultural Study in the Deep South* 173 (1939).
12. *Brown v. Board of Education*, 347 U.S. 483 (1954).
13. See generally Klarman, *supra* note 7, Chapter 7.
14. Loic Wacquant, *Punishing the Poor: The Neoliberal Government of Social Insecurity* 68 (2009).
15. Id. at 7.
16. Michelle Alexander, *The New Jim Crow: Mass Incarceration in the Age of Colorblindness* xiv (rev. ed., 2020).
17. Michelle Alexander, "Reckoning with Violence," *The New York Times*, March 3, 2019.
18. Id.

CHAPTER 4

Utopian Possibilities

During the summer of 2020, shortly after George Floyd's death at the hands of four Minneapolis police officers, major publications started to give serious attention to what had previously been fringe movements in criminal law—one known as *defund the police*, the other as *prison abolition*. As for the first, *The New York Times* published an opinion piece by Miriame Kaba in which she rejected what she called the "procedural tweaks" proposed by criminal law reformers and declared that the time had come to defund the police altogether. "We don't just want to close police departments. We want to make them obsolete," she wrote.

> We should redirect the billions that now go to police departments toward providing health care, housing, education. If we did this, we'd have less need for the police in the first place. We can build other ways of responding to harms in our society. Trained "community care workers" could do mental-health checks if someone needs help. Towns could use restorative-justice models instead of throwing people in prison.[1]

Kaba's *defund the police* proposal was complemented by arguments for *prison abolition*. More than a decade and half before George Floyd's death, Angela Davis stated that "prisons are an obsolete institution because they exacerbate societal harms instead of fixing them."[2] More recently, Allegra McLeod built on Davis's position in an article published

W. C. Heffernan, *Social Justice/Criminal Justice*,
https://doi.org/10.1007/978-3-031-75397-8_4

in the *Harvard Law Review*, urging "the complete and utter dismantling of prisons, policing, and surveillance as they currently exist within our culture." Abolitionists "understand their work to be related to the historical struggles against slavery and its afterlives," McLeod stated, "against imperialism and its legacies in more recent practices of racial capitalism, and against immigration enforcement and border fortification." On McLeod's account, abolitionism holds out the prospect of "grounded justice." It looks forward to the prospect of a genuinely just social order—and thus looks forward to the gradual abolition of the entire apparatus of domination essential to the administration of criminal law.[3]

There are important qualifiers contained in each of the proposals just quoted—think, for example, about Kaba's "less need for the police" and contrast this with the possibility of *no need whatsoever* and, similarly, consider McLeod's proposal to dismantle prisons and police forces "as they currently exist within our culture" and contrast this with the possibility of *dismantling prisons and police entirely*. If we set these qualifiers aside for a moment, we can see that commentators like Kaba and McLeod might say that the decent society framework proposed in the earlier chapters suffers from a lack of imagination. Promoting social justice will make criminal justice completely unnecessary, they might say. If we think in a genuinely bold way, they imply, there will be no need to reason in terms of a *connection* between social justice and criminal justice, for once the full requisites of social justice are provided, criminal justice will become obsolete.

Needless to say, the qualifiers just noted indicate that these utopian possibilities are mere intimations: they aren't anticipated with certainty. "Less need for the police" and dismantlement of criminal justice agencies "as they currently exist" are formulae that allow for leeway about what communal life will be like in the socially just world that may (or may not) emerge. Given the importance of these qualifiers, it would be unreasonable to say that the passages just quoted are entirely incompatible with the more sober, non-utopian notion of a decent society proposed in earlier chapters. This said, though, there is an obvious contrast—a contrast in rhetoric and terminology but also a contrast in programmatic content—that distinguishes the notion of a decent society outlined earlier from the notion of penal abolition that informs the commentary just quoted. In speaking of a decent society, someone allows for the likelihood that crime will continue to occur (and that it sometimes will continue to be punished) *even with* the satisfactory provision of social justice. In speaking of abolition, on the other hand, someone anticipates (without insisting on the inevitability of) a world in which a central enforcement agency will no longer be needed since there will no longer be acts of *WFF* that require the community's attention.

This chapter examines both approaches. It does so in three sections, each concerned with the tension between visionary conceptions of a socially just world that can dispense entirely with coercive enforcement of the obligations of restraint and a world of incremental reforms that accept the necessity of criminal justice. Although the argument here favors the latter over the former, the chapter focuses on visions of a wholly just social order—visions that may never be fulfilled—which inform conclusions about the state's response to harmful acts. Utopia is unlikely to be achieved. This doesn't mean, though, that we should be indifferent to its allure.

Utopian vs. Scientific Socialism

In the final chapter of *The Communist Manifesto*, Karl Marx and Friedrich Engels introduce the term *utopian socialism* to discuss the ideas of political commentators—Robert Owen and Pierre-Joseph Proudhon, for instance—who imagine what communal life will be like following the end of capitalism. *The Manifesto* is by no means entirely dismissive of these writers' ideas. Utopian socialists anticipate "the disappearance of class antagonisms," Marx and Engels note; they envision a future of "social harmony [and] the conversion of the functions of the state into a mere superintendence of production…." These anticipations are welcome components of the class struggle, Marx and Engels contend: they're "valuable materials for the enlightenment of the working class." Because the writings of utopian socialists "attack every principle of existing society," they have the potential to inspire those oppressed by the current order.[4]

But while *The Manifesto's* authors welcome the rhetoric of utopian socialism, they're careful to emphasize that their goals are fundamentally different. The *Manifesto's* central concern, after all, is to explain *how* to bring about the class struggle: it isn't to outline *what* the new order will be like but instead to disrupt the current one. The *Manifesto* thus dismisses Owen, Proudhon, et al. as authors who provide "fantastic pictures of future society, painted at a time when the proletariat is still in a very undeveloped state…." By contrast, Marx and Engels trace the likely course of socialist development, explain how that development will culminate in the birth of a classless society, and, in particular, provide strategic guidance for the revolutionary struggle that will bring about this painful birth. "The significance of critical-utopian socialism and communism bears an inverse relation to historical development," they write. "In proportion as the modern class struggle develops and takes definite shape, this fantastic standing apart from the contest, these fantastic attacks on it, lose all practical value and theoretical significance."[5] Marx and Engels don't "stand [] apart" from the class struggle; they write from within it.

Marx thus emphasizes that his historically specific vantage point makes it possible for him to analyze capitalism's internal contradictions and to engage in strategic deliberations for overthrowing it but that it doesn't provide him with privileged insight into the details of the classless society to come. Nonetheless, Marx occasionally sets aside this self-imposed limitation. When he does so, his comments have a distinctly utopian air to them. His remarks in *Critique of the Gotha Program*, written more than a quarter century after the *Manifesto*, underscore this point. "In a higher phase of communist society," Marx states,

> after the enslaving subordination of the individual to the division of labor, ... [and] after labor has become not only a means of life but life's prime want, after the productive forces have increased with the all-round development of the individual, and all the springs of co-operative wealth flow more abundantly, only then can the narrow horizon of bourgeois right be crossed in its entirety and society inscribe on its banner: From each according to his ability, to each according to his needs.[6]

As the recurrent use of the word *after* indicates here, Marx allows himself in this passage to look beyond the present—to transcend "the narrow horizon of bourgeois right," as he puts it—and so to glimpse a further, as yet non-existent, stage of human development. Few of his writings contain comments of this kind, however. By and large, his writings and those of Engels focus on means rather than ends—and so avoid speculation about world that has yet to emerge.

Indeed, following Marx's death, Engels went a step further and insisted that both of them were proponents of scientific rather than utopian socialism. Like Marx, Engels offers occasional glimpses of the future. In particular, his later commentary anticipates the "withering away of the state" once the class struggle has been successfully waged.[7] As a general rule, though, Engels's later remarks focus on the *how* questions associated with scientific socialism rather than the *what* questions associated with its utopian counterpart. Scientific socialism, Engels claims, provides leaders of the revolution with the technical knowledge to bring about concrete change in human relations.[8] It stays away from what he and Marx called "fantastic pictures of future society." Instead, it deals rationally with the complex details of altering the structure of social relations, thereby *making* obsolete "the narrow horizon of bourgeois right" rather than simply *announcing* that this has become obsolete.

Holding People Accountable for their Harmful Acts

Almost exactly a century after Marx wrote *Critique of the Gotha Program*, Richard Quinney applied Marxist reasoning to criminal law in *Critique of Legal Order: Crime Control in Capitalist Society*. Quinney's core claims can be captured in three propositions. (1) "The state is organized to serve the interests of the dominant economic class, the capitalist ruling class." (2) "Criminal law is an instrument of the state and ruling class to maintain and perpetuate the existing social and economic order." And (3) "Only with the collapse of capitalist society and the creation of a new society, based on socialist principles, will there be a solution to the crime problem."[9]

The first two of these propositions, if updated to include concerns with race, can easily be reconciled with the dystopian arguments about state capture examined in the previous chapter. The third goes beyond them: it anticipates, in rhetoric that's more than faintly utopian, "a solution to the crime problem," one that will emerge from a "collapse" of the old order and "the creation of a new society." Quinney is less forthcoming than Marx and Engels about *how* this collapse will come about. And he is certainly just as vague as his predecessors as to *what* the new society will be like. Will the solution to the crime problem occur because human predation will disappear—because the harmonious social relations Marx anticipates in *Critique of the Gotha Program* will make it unnecessary even to think about harmful acts and thus unnecessary to think about criminal justice? Or will the solution occur because the state will no longer be the enforcement arm of the ruling class—because it will "wither away" in its current form, to draw on Engels's term (though with the qualifier *in its current form*), thus making it possible to establish a central enforcement agency that responds impartially to harmful acts as these continue to occur even after the collapse of capitalism?

Questions along these lines are inescapably important for *defund the police* and *prison abolition* advocates. The former question is concerned with genuinely utopian possibilities. It dispenses with the qualifiers that, as noted earlier in this chapter, often accompany arguments for dismantling criminal justice institutions. The latter question, on the other hand, takes those qualifiers seriously. It presupposes the key point discussed in the latter chapter: the ongoing possibility of state power (*coercive* power, manifested in acts of domination and submission), with that power deployed to hold people accountable for what they've done. It presupposes nothing more than this preliminary feature of grievance-redress. As noted in the previous chapter, a procedural requirement that calls on suspects to account for their conduct doesn't presuppose the continued existence of prisons; it doesn't even presuppose that punishment will be imposed when one person harms another.

But the second question does presuppose an institution that exercises dominant force in investigating the circumstances of harmful conduct. Although many *defund/abolish* commentators sidestep questions about accountability (no further government investigation into sexual abuse of minors? into claims of violent rape? into claims of commercial fraud?), some do not. Allegra McLeod, for example, argues for elimination of "existing punitive institutions while identifying meaningful forms of accountability to respond to actual violence and wrongdoing."[10] McLeod doesn't explain what she means by *meaningful forms of accountability*, but given her reference to violence and wrongdoing, it's clear in this context, as it was in the context of Alexander's remarks, that this kind of accountability necessarily includes the exercise of coercive power by state officials—and thus the mastery/submission dynamic used to effectuate an arrest and to investigate the circumstances associated with a harmful act. Because other *defund/abolish* commentators support programs such as restorative justice and civil restitution,[11] they too can be taken to support, at least by implication, the use of coercive power by a central enforcement agency that initiates inquiry into individual accountability.

The points just made, it should be emphasized, do not mean that *defund/abolish* advocates support state-imposed punishment (McLeod's remarks concerning this can't be ignored). Nonetheless, they make clear acceptance of the importance of the most basic of all features of criminal justice—that an impartial authority (self-interested forms of retaliation of the *lex talionis* type are thus unacceptable) must be vested with coercive power to begin the process of holding people accountable for the harm they may have brought about.

On this reckoning, a further qualification of the points made in the previous chapter is needed, a qualification that rejects the *superfluousness thesis* concerning criminal justice. On MacLeod's reckoning *even when* the government provides the full measure of social justice, it *also* has a critical role to play in ensuring criminal justice. In particular, on the analysis just provided, social justice makes criminal justice less necessary, but it doesn't make criminal justice obsolete. Criminal justice is always essential (on non-utopian accounts, at least), though it's essential only because prevention of violations of the obligations of restraint is an inescapable feature of communal life and because institutions of accountability must have the power to require people charged with harming others to answer for their conduct. Commentary that avoids this point is escapist in that it evades a recurrent, and tragic, feature of human relations. At a minimum, any credible (non-ideal) theory of justice must offer details as to the institutions that can properly be used to call on people to account for the harm they have done to others.

The argument just made about the importance of the demand for accountability has a bearing on John Rawls's insistence on limiting his commentary on justice to ideal theory. A premise of ideal theory is that all members of society are prepared to comply with the fair terms of cooperation—and thus that none will violate the obligations of restraint which sustain fair cooperation. On Rawls's account, this vision of social life is "realistically utopian"[12]—not wholly *un*realistic, he seems to think, but sufficiently beyond the limits of everyday self-restraint that he doesn't contemplate establishment of a central enforcement agency to call on suspects to account for their conduct.

But while Rawls takes refuge in the paradoxical term *realistically utopian* here, we can see that he, too, falls back on something akin to utopian reasoning, for it is *not* realistic—indeed, it's incompatible with what we know about life among higher primates generally—to disregard the non-ideal insights available to us about the possibility of aggression and the possibility of deterring it by calling on people to account for their conduct. To note this is not to undervalue ideal theory. Rather, it's to insist, as does the argument advanced throughout the book, on the complementarity of ideal theory (as the avenue to reflection on the principles of social justice) and non-ideal theory (as the avenue to reflection on the principles of criminal justice).

Social Justice Within and Beyond Criminal Justice

The points just made have ramifications for criminal justice as a standalone concept and also for the social justice/criminal justice connection. Consider first their implications for criminal justice on its own, in particular their implications for accountability and punishment.

If we assume that the Constitution's due process standards satisfactorily identify a fact-finder's obligation to evaluate grievances impartially (and agree that any accountability procedure involves a relationship of domination in which one person exercises mastery over another to investigate an incident), we can further say that some degree of force is needed to ensure the proper functioning of a system of criminal justice. The amount of force to be employed should be no greater than that which is needed to ensure the possibility of effective inquiry into the circumstances surrounding a harmful act. Given this point, one can't endorse *defund the police* if that slogan is understood as a categorical one. We can of course agree with Mariame Koba that there should be "less need for the police." It's the further step—categorical dismissal of policing as a feature of a just society—that can't be taken.

Is punishment *also* a necessary component of criminal justice? It can readily be agreed that punishment amounts to a different, and more troubling, form of domination than the kind needed to hold someone accountable for harm. Because this is so, it might be argued that punishment isn't needed even though institutions of accountability are indispensable. After all, there are many alternatives to punishment when harm has occurred. Restitution may be sufficient as a matter of justice. If it isn't, the reconciliation process employed in restorative justice settings may prove satisfactory.

It would be unwise, however, to reject punishment altogether for cases of grave wrongdoing. Rather than repudiate it entirely, the sounder approach is to say that punishment should be disfavored as long as some other option proves satisfactory. And, in any event, even if punishment is employed, it can be added that imprisonment (enhanced punishment, we might say) should be disfavored when some other form of surveillance—electronic supervision, for instance—is feasible. Punishment shouldn't be rejected entirely, then; even if imprisonment shouldn't be wholly rejected. On the other hand, a framework that treats it as disfavored must also be adopted in order to promote its parsimonious use.

These comments about accountability and punishment apply to criminal justice generally. They're indirectly pertinent to social justice because the apparatus of state penal power has so often been used to perpetrate social injustice. Now let us turn to the social justice/criminal justice connection—i.e., to those settings in which social justice matters *within* the operation of criminal law (since it reduces racial and class disparities in legal outcomes) and *beyond* the law's operation (since it contributes more generally to the creation of a decent society).

The rationale for pursuing social justice initiatives within the legal system is straightforward. Even if the requisites of social justice aren't met in the community at large (even if a society is problematic, in other words), it's essential at a minimum to adopt measures that aim at purging vestiges of social injustice from the legal process. To put this point differently, we can say that in the midst of a problematic communal order (an order where the requisites of social justice haven't been provided but where the procedural requisites of criminal justice remain in reach since the pathology of state capture no longer exists), it's still imperative to address issues such as racialized policing, inadequate provision of counsel for indigent defendants, and racial disparities in criminal sentencing. *Within* issues such as these are affronts to an elementary principle of justice: they're affronts to the EO principle of treating like cases alike. To return to the term introduced in the previous chapter when discussing Alexander's work, they're *something* issues. Granted, they don't ensure *everything*—that is, they have only a tangential connection to a socially just communal order. On the other hand, they can't reasonably be dismissed as *nothing*.

Within reasoning is concerned primarily with questions of fairness—with treating like cases alike and thus ensuring that the outcomes of the criminal process aren't tainted by morally arbitrary factors related to someone's birth. This is important in itself. A decent society aims at more than this, however. It seeks as well to ensure full provision of social justice beyond the legal system, and to the extent this goal is attained, its achievement will have positive repercussions on the system's internal operation. These repercussions can include the following: limitations on the scope of the criminal law (in particular, measures that limit it to prohibitions on wrongful, force, and fraud), adoption of rules that prevent prosperous members of a community from insulating themselves from criminal liability, establishment of a framework that promotes parsimonious use of punishment and that therefore guards against the possibility against mass incarceration, and measures that promote equal social standing. Each of these is a proactive step: each, in other words, is designed to ensure that a decent society uses the criminal sanction sparingly and also that its organs of power aren't deployed to shore up the privileged position of some groups by comparison with others. It's in this sense that trends beyond the legal system—trends that promote social justice in the community at large—can beneficially alter the system's internal operation.

It's possible to reframe the *within/beyond* contrast by returning to the distinction between a problematic and decent society. Social justice considerations can be incorporated into the operation of the legal system even when the society it serves hasn't satisfied the full requisites of social justice. In contrast, the *beyond* initiatives mentioned above require a community-wide commitment to social justice—a commitment to a decent society, one in which the structure of social justice informs the operation of all the major institutions of the community. If and when there is such a commitment, adherence to it can be expected to move from outside to inside, thereby affecting positively the operation of the legal system.

The two sections that follow evaluate the administration of criminal law by reference to the *within/beyond* distinction just outlined. The chapters in Section III consider issues internal to criminal law—racial disparities in stop-question-frisk; class disparities in access to the courts; and racial and gender disparities in sentencing. The chapters in Section IV address structural issues—the importance of a general commitment to limiting criminal law to prohibitions on *WFF*; the need to make sure that prosperous members of society can't leverage their social standing to avoid, or at least minimize, criminal liability (particularly with regard to taxes); and the imperative of addressing mass incarceration through adoption of a commitment to penal parsimony in the legal system and a commitment to wealth redistribution in society at large. Adoption of the Section III proposals would make the internal operation of the legal system less problematic. Adoption of the proposals in the later section as well would hold out the prospect of the creation of a decent society.

Notes

1. Miriame Kaba, "Yes, We Mean Literally Abolish the Police," *The New York Times*, June 14, 2020 SR 2.
2. This remark by Angela Davis is quoted in John Washington, "What Is Prison Abolition?" *Nation*, July 31, 2018. See also Davis's *Is Prison Obsolete?* (2003).
3. Allegra McLeod, "Envisioning Abolition Democracy," *Harvard Law Review* 132: 1613, 1616 (2019).
4. Karl Marx and Friedrich Engels, *The Communist Manifesto* [1848] in *The Marx-Engels Reader*, Robert Tucker, ed. 497–98 (Second ed. 1978).
5. Id.
6. Karl Marx, *Critique of the Gotha Program* [1875] in id. 531.
7. V.I. Lenin quotes Engels as follows: "The state will not be 'abolished'; it will wither away." Lenin, *The State and Revolution* 20 (1919), citing Engels's *Herr Eugen Duhrings Umwalzung der Wissenschaft* [1878].
8. See Engels's *Socialism: Utopian and Scientific* [1880] in Tucker, *supra* note 3, at 683.
9. Richard Quinney, *Critique of Legal Order: Crime Control in Capitalist Society* 15–16 (1974).
10. McLeod, *supra* note 3, at 1616–17.
11. See, e.g., Washington, *supra* note 2, for arguments in favor of restorative justice and civil restitution by advocates of prison abolition.
12. Rawls, *supra* note 7 in Introduction.

PART III

Addressing Social Justice Issues Within the Criminal Law

CHAPTER 5

Addressing Racial Disparities in Police Use of Force

As noted in the first chapter, the criminal process typically originates in a dynamic of domination and submission, one in which an official makes a showing of authority and a suspect bows to this by curtailing his/her freedom of movement. The criminal process doesn't always originate in this way, though. After all, a suspect may refuse to submit, and when this happens submission is often replaced by something more drastic—by subjugation through brute force, perhaps even by subjugation through the use of deadly force.

Is this domination/submission dynamic emblematic of injustice in society at large? Someone skeptical of the very exercise of the state's exercise of coercive power might advance an argument along these lines, at least with regard to the exercise of authority by a police officer over a suspect from an impoverished background, for then the dynamic could be said to symbolize the massed power of the state over those who've been denied the requisites of social justice. To take this position, though, is to disregard the possibility that the person being detained may have violated one of the obligations of restraint—and so to disregard the state's unique role in vindicating violations of those obligations by calling on the suspect to account for what he/she has done.

Because this is a possibility that can't immediately be dismissed—because it's essential to consider scenarios in which a state that's failed

W. C. Heffernan, *Social Justice/Criminal Justice*,
https://doi.org/10.1007/978-3-031-75397-8_5

to provide the requisites of social justice may nonetheless have an important role to play in vindicating the obligations of restraint—this chapter and the two that follow consider a more nuanced possibility. That is, the three chapters in this section focus on shortcomings *within* the administration of criminal law that disadvantage already-disadvantaged members of society. In particular, this chapter focuses on racial disparities in police practices that leave African-Americans and Hispanics at a substantial disadvantage under the law (while the next two chapters deal with class and racial disparities elsewhere in the legal system). The core premise of all three chapters is straightforward: even if people haven't otherwise received the requisites of social justice, the chapters suggest, they at least shouldn't be further disadvantaged by government actions as a result of their background.

Unfortunately, they are—or at least they are in many instances. That is, in examining data concerning police interventions, we will see that racial minorities are often treated less well than other citizens when officers conduct stop-question-and-frisk and when they make arrests. These conclusions aren't based on anecdotes. Rather, they are supported by surveys of patterns of practice that have unfolded in accordance with legal norms over the course of the preceding quarter century. They are findings about institutionally authorized exercises of discretion, in other words—findings which establish that patterns of injustice in society at large infect the administration of criminal law, thereby worsening the plight of those already disadvantaged by the distribution of goods and services. Given this macro-social effect, the findings give rise to challenging questions about the steps that should be taken to eliminate the unjustified disparities affecting contemporary policing.

The chapter that follows is divided into three sections. The first examines the unquestionable social benefits generated by policing. The next two sections consider two problematic features of contemporary police practice—one having to do with stop-question-and-frisk, the other with the use of force in conducting arrests. The inquiry undertaken is rooted in empirical research. In building on this, it outlines remedial steps that could be taken to address the unacceptable effects of racial disparities in contemporary policing.

The Redistributive Benefits of Policing

We should start with a positive point, one that can be expressed by thinking about class as well as racial disparities. This is that, given the fact that the administration of criminal law is paid for through tax revenues, disadvantaged members of society benefit disproportionately from its operation. Magnus Lofstrom and Steven Raphael succinctly express this point. Over the past three to four decades, they write, "crime rates declined the most in poorer and more minority cities, and within cities in the poorest neighborhoods." Because the poor pay a smaller percentage of their income in taxes than do members of the higher classes, the authors write, "the benefit of the crime decline [since the late twentieth century] has been progressively distributed."[1] Public safety—in the form of protection from violent crimes such as murder, rape, and robbery—has been achieved *redistributively*, in other words: taxes paid by prosperous members of society disproportionately have aided its less prosperous members.

At stake here is an unequivocally important social good. Even if we grant (as we must given the fact that Lofstrom and Raphael, like virtually all criminologists, are *not* concerned with the final *F*—i.e., fraud—in *WFF* but only with *WF*) that the point just made does not extend to all criminal acts, we must also grant that protecting people from *WF* is essential to a decent society. And, given the authors' findings, we also must grant that this good is achieved by means of the redistributive measures essential to social justice. The disadvantaged pay *less* than they otherwise would for the protection they receive from the state-as-central-enforcement-agency; in turn, prosperous members of society pay more than they otherwise would for the same services.

Needless to say, there is a flip side to the proposition just noted, for Lofstrom and Raphael add that "the social costs created by the unprecedented expansion in correctional populations have been regressively distributed, with poor, disproportionately minority males (African-American males in particular) being the most directly impacted and poor minority families (again African-American families) disproportionately bearing the collateral social costs of the stiffening of US sentencing policy."[2] This flip side can't be ignored; indeed, it's the central concern of virtually all the chapters in this book. But the positive point can't be ignored either, and it's essential to note it at the beginning of our empirical survey, for it underscores the subtlety of the issues associated with the social justice/criminal justice connection. Without noting that the state-as-central-enforcement agency protects lives while also degrading them unnecessarily, we would fail to come to terms with what is essentially sound about the contemporary administration of criminal law—even if our attention will be devoted primarily to what's *un*sound.

It's possible to add to this point: to note that the public might benefit more (and that the disadvantaged would particularly benefit more under the redistributive framework just outlined) with the addition of more police personnel. This is because it can reasonably be argued that American cities are under-, not over-, policed. That is, if a dollar value is assigned to individual lives and a dollar value is also assigned to the cost of expanding the police force, there is strong evidence to believe that the extra investment in personnel would provide cost-effective savings in promoting personal security. A 2013 estimate along these lines suggested, for instance, that each dollar spent would reduce victim costs by $1.63[3]—a substantial saving not only in monetary terms but, when translated into human ones, an impressive one when consideration is given to the suffering that might be avoided.

Racial Disparities in Stop-Question-and-Frisk

But this argument about underpolicing is advanced without regard to the burdens occasioned by racial disparities in police interventions in individual lives. What if the economically or racially disadvantaged come out better as far as lives saved are concerned but worse as far as dignity in police encounters is concerned? There's no objective metric that can answer this question—no way, in other words, to calculate the net benefit, or net loss, generated by discriminatory policing as opposed to extra safety. What can be said, though, is that a decent society is possible only when safeguards are adopted that minimize unnecessary police interventions *while also* promoting personal safety.

On this reckoning, contemporary policing is less than satisfactory. New York City's experience with stop-question-and-frisk (SQF) offers a helpful way to understand why. Under rules the Supreme Court has established for SQF, police officers are permitted to detain suspects (on the street, when driving, and when traveling in other public places such as airports and train stations) for brief investigation on the basis of reasonable suspicion that a crime has been committed, is being committed, or is about to be committed. This *reasonable suspicion* standard is lower than the one for arrests, the standard for which is *probable cause*. Because the standard is lower, the scope of a police intervention must be more limited than for arrests—more limited in time (i.e., only a brief encounter is permitted) and also more limited in scope (through a frisk for weapons as distinguished from a full-blown search for weapons and evidence of a crime).[4]

The SQF rules outlined above are race- (and class-) neutral. This doesn't mean, though, that the rules have been *applied* neutrally. Table 1, which reviews New York City's experience with SQF under three twenty-first-century mayors, illustrates this point. The table does so by examining two different features of police interventions, one having to do with the ethnicity of those stopped and frisked, the other with "hit rates" during stops. Each reveals the potential for biased application of rules that vest officers with discretion in race- and class-neutral terms. Think first about the ethnicity of those detained. Although New York City is approximately 50% Black and Hispanic, about 85% of twenty-first-century NYPD SQFs were carried out on members of these two ethnic groups.

Might this disparity be justified on the ground that Blacks and Hispanics commit more violent crime than Whites—or, at least, that the disproportionate burden borne by ethnic minorities was properly placed on them given the effect of their crime rates on city life? A rationale along the latter line was proposed in the later years of the Bloomberg administration. The data don't bear it out, however. On the contrary, SQF declined—declined more than 90% under Mayor DeBlasio. But *index crimes declined as well.* It's true that index crimes increased somewhat under Mayor Adams. This can reasonably be attributed to the worldwide uptick in COVID-related crime in the early 2020s, though, so as a general matter, we can say that SQF in New York City wasn't simply *un*productive as far as index crime was concerned, it was *counter*productive in that it burdened Blacks and Hispanics without reducing the rate of index crime.

And what about disparities in the hit rate? Here, the results are more straightforward: police consistently had to stop and frisk more Blacks and Hispanics than they did Whites to gain the same amount of contraband. SQF was less efficient—more intrusive, more humiliating—for one group rather than another, in other words. All this through discretionary application of race- and class-neutral rules!

Is there a way to remedy this? Two answers are possible, one more radical than the other. The modest approach involves more careful monitoring of police behavior. In response to a lawsuit concerning the constitutionality of its SQF program, for instance, the NYPD now has a quality-control team that examines officers' implementation of SQF, a team that, among other things, examines video footage from body-worn cameras and adopts training lessons designed to correct common police errors. This remedial step holds out the prospect of incremental improvement. It accepts the legitimacy of SQF while seeking to make it less burdensome for those most affected by it.[5]

The more far-reaching approach is to forgo SQF completely. Constitutional blessing for it came in a Supreme Court case that's only slightly more than a half-century old. The opinion in that case granted that ethnic minorities bear the brunt of police interventions. The intervening years have demonstrated that this is a sound point. Moreover, the contrast between the Bloomberg and DeBlasio years in New York City demonstrates that SQF may not contribute substantially to reduction in index crimes. At the least, it seems that the time has come for a police department to experiment with no SQF whatsoever. The time may have come, in other words, to return to the constitutional standard that existed for the first century and three quarters of American history—a standard that treats probable cause, not reasonable suspicion, as decisive and that therefore protects everyone in his/her freedom of movement absent substantial evidence of wrongdoing.

Use of Force and Deadly Force in Probable Cause Settings

Even if this more radical remedy were adopted, one would still have to ask whether Blacks and Hispanics are more burdened by an exclusive reliance on probable cause than are Whites. The data are quite clear that the disadvantaged also experience a more substantial burden even here, for probable cause has long served as the criterion for arrest. Surprisingly, the data are less clear with respect to deadly force. Each point merits consideration on its own.

Think first about questions concerned with nonlethal force. This, of course, is the term to use when considering the domination/submission dynamic associated with arrest in its standard form, for when a police officer takes someone into custody, the suspect signals acceptance of the officer's authority by an act of submission and the officer responds to this by using the minimum amount of force needed to secure ongoing restraint. This race-neutral formula cannot, however, be translated into a race-neutral account of the outcomes of police arrests. On the contrary, as Roland Fryer notes in summarizing the results of a study of nearly five million police-citizen encounters, "[t]here are large racial differences in police use of nonlethal force." In drawing on a nationally representative dataset asking people about their encounters with the police, Fryer reports that his research team "found the use of physical force on blacks to be 350% more likely" than it is for whites. "This is true of every level of nonlethal force," Fryer writes, "from officers putting their hands on civilians to striking them with batons. We controlled for every variable in myriad ways. That reduced disparities by 66%, but blacks were still significantly more likely to endure physical force."[6]

What about compliance? Suspects often fail to comply with officers' exercise of authority, so it's essential to ask whether racial disparities in *non*-compliance are reflected in racial disparities in the exercise of nonlethal force. Even when this question is posed, though, Fryer found substantial differences that correlate with race. "Black civilians who were recorded as compliant by police were 21% more likely to suffer police aggression than compliant police," Fryer writes.

> This was perhaps our most upsetting result, for two reasons: The inequity in spite of compliance clashed with the notion that the difference in police treatment of blacks and whites was a rational response to danger. And it complicates what we tell our kids: Compliance makes you less likely to endure a beat-down—but the benefit is larger if you are white.[7]

Fryer's conclusions about nonlethal force are compatible with other findings about police behavior. Because they are, they can be said to establish conclusively that, in early twenty-first-century America, the social justice deficits associated with the general structure of communal life also infect the administration of criminal law. Those who are disadvantaged in their quest for jobs and housing are further disadvantaged in their encounters with officials who administer the law.

And what about lethal force? What about disparities in the use of deadly force, guns in particular, when there's probable cause to arrest and a police allegation of resistance that might justify lethal violence in order to assert police authority? It's understandable that anecdotes—about Laquan McDonald, a Black teenager shot 16 times by a Chicago police officer and George Floyd, a middle-aged Black man who died by asphyxiation as Minneapolis officers held him down—tend to frame public debate concerning this. Our concern is patterns of practice, however, not harrowing individual incidents, and once this statistical perspective is adopted, we find that researchers have reached differing, and incompatible, conclusions concerning lethal force.

Roland Fryer stands on one side of this divide. While finding strong evidence of racial disparities in compliance with arrests that aren't backed up by lethal force, Fryer did not discern such disparities when the force at stake is deadly. "No matter how we analyzed our data, we found no racial differences in shootings overall, in any city in particular, or in any subset of the data," Fryer writes. Recognizing that this conclusion may occasion surprise, Fryer adds that his research focuses on statistics, not specific incidents. "It isn't average when a police officer casually kneels on someone's neck for 8 minutes and 46 seconds [a reference to George Floyd's death-by–asphyxiation]," he comments. "Are there racial differences in the most extreme forms of police violence? The Southern boy in me says yes; the economist says we don't know."[8]

Fryer's *we don't know* has been met with considerable criticism, largely because of the methodology he employed in reaching his conclusions. That methodology relies on data provided by police departments, not on data generated by means of independent research. In drawing on this source, Fryer turns to statistics that "underestimate or conceal entirely the differential police violence faced by civilians of color," Dean Knox and his colleagues argue. In turning to non-police sources, Knox et al. contend that Fryer underestimates by as much as 40% police applications of lethal force. Fryer's "naïve approach" to methodological issues, Knox and his colleagues maintain, fails to come to terms with the special burdens posed by legal authorization of police use of deadly force.[9] Because lethal force is of greater importance than anything else as far as the police are concerned, this charge has to be taken very seriously.

Is it accurate, though—and should Fryer's finding concerning deadly force be set aside? At present, there's no clear way to arbitrate this disagreement. Because Knox et al. rely on sources that also may be suspect, it's impossible to reach a firm conclusion here. What can be said, however, is that more systematic monitoring of police use of deadly force is needed *even if* Fryer's more favorable conclusion is reached, for whatever the soundness of the Knox criticisms, it's undeniable that lethal force must be scrutinized with the greatest care by all police departments. At stake here is an issue of national significance, one that not only should give rise to minimum standards for the use of deadly force but also to legislation (passed pursuant to Congress's power to regulate interstate commerce) that creates a regulatory authority that oversees police use of deadly force. At present, there is no such legislation. It's urgently needed given the importance of the issue under consideration.

Notes

1. Lofstrom and Raphael, "Crime, the Criminal Justice System, and Socioeconomic Inequality," *Journal of Economic Perspectives* 30 (2): 103, 117 (2016).
2. Id. 104.
3. Chalfin and McCrary, "Are U.S. Cities Underpoliced? Theory and Evidence," *The Review of Economics and Statistics* 100 (1): 167, 184 (2018).
4. See *Terry v. Ohio*, 392 U.S. 1 (1968).
5. See *Floyd* et al. *v. City of New York*, 959 F. Supp. 2d 540 (S.D.N.Y, 2013).
6. Roland Fryer Jr., "An Empirical Analysis of Racial Differences in Police Use of Force," *Journal of Political Economy*, 127 (3): 1210 (2019).
7. Roland Fryer Jr., "What the Data Say About Police," *Wall Street Journal*, June 22, 2020.
8. Id.
9. Dean Knox et al., "Administrative Records Mask Racially Biased Policing," *American Political Science Review*, 114 (3): 619, 620 (2020).

CHAPTER 6

Addressing Class Disparities: Promoting Equal Access to Legal Proceedings

In 1963, the Supreme Court ruled in *Gideon v. Wainwright* that a defendant may not be convicted of a felony without having been offered the aid of a lawyer. *Gideon* was a constitutional case; it relied on the Sixth Amendment's text, which states that "[i]n all criminal cases, the accused shall have … the assistance of counsel in his defence," to justify its conclusion. The *Gideon* Court didn't say that the state must pay for a lawyer when a defendant is too poor to pay for one him/herself. Rather, it held, if only by implication, that a social justice principle is essential to criminal justice. Indeed, *Gideon* held (though, again, only by implication) that social justice takes priority over the administration of criminal law, for an inescapable ramification of *Gideon* is that in the absence of a state offer to provide assistance of counsel (or a defendant's knowing waiver of this), government cannot prevail.[1] No similar principle governs the operation of civil law. Only when the criminal process is set in motion is the state required to offer to pay for an attorney if it is to prevail in a legal proceeding.

Given this social justice principle, *Gideon* can be said to address a class issue concerning the administration of criminal law. Because there are racial disparities in the distribution of wealth, it's a near certainty that Blacks and Hispanics benefit disproportionately from *Gideon*. This said, though, *Gideon* makes sense only as a case concerned with class. It's a case that seeks—imperfectly—to correct for wealth disparities (regardless

W. C. Heffernan, *Social Justice/Criminal Justice*,
https://doi.org/10.1007/978-3-031-75397-8_6

of race) by promoting universal access to the procedural rights essential to criminal law. So understood, *Gideon* can be said to aim at making wealth irrelevant to legal outcomes in the criminal process. It stands for the general principle that a just deprivation of liberty is possible only if someone charged with a crime has a fair equality of opportunity to receive subsided aid that will make it possible to mount a meaningful challenge against the government's effort to deprive him/her of liberty.

What is the scope of this general principle—the *Gideon* principle, as we can call it? Does it cover all crimes for which a defendant might be charged, misdemeanors as well as felonies? Does it mandate financial assistance for incidental features of criminal defense work? For example, does it mandate state financial assistance to conduct criminal investigation that supports an alibi defense? Does it guarantee subsidies for an independent psychiatric evaluation if a defendant suffers from a mental disorder? Does it cover cash bail, also a class (rather than a race) issue, but one that's covered by the Eighth Amendment's prohibition of excessive bail rather than the Sixth Amendment's assistance of counsel clause? The answer to these questions is *no, no,* and *no*—or (to qualify these points): the assistance of counsel clause has not been held to cover *all* criminal prosecutions; it has not been held to provide across-the-board assistance for investigative or psychiatric services; and given the Eighth Amendment's bail reference,[2] neither *Gideon* nor anything remotely connected to it can be said to address the issue of cash bail. At most, then, *Gideon* states a principle concerning fair equalization of opportunity for criminal defendants. In practice, though, that principle has limited reach, thus making for substantial social justice deficits in the administration of criminal law since well-off criminal defendants can draw on their own resources and so answer *yes, yes,* and *yes* to each of the questions just posed.

This chapter addresses the social justice deficits just noted. It first considers equalizing issues associated with the practice of cash bail. It then turns to assistance of counsel. The questions at stake are fundamentally different, for bail decisions are predictive in nature (they ask about the risk a defendant poses before he/she is placed on trial), whereas assistance of counsel issues center on classic questions about the equalization of state resources. Both subjects come under the heading of class rather than race, though. Moreover, both are concerned with questions about fairness. As will be seen, there is a great deal more that could be done with respect to each issue—a great deal more, in other words, that could be done to ensure that wealth plays no role in determining the outcomes of the criminal process.

Bail

Because the criminal process originates in an act of domination, one of the first questions that arises once a suspect has been charged with a crime is whether that person is to be released from government restraint prior to trial. In Anglo-American law, release operates by a system known as *bail*. Bail, William Blackstone wrote in his *Commentaries on the Laws of England*, published in the 1760s, consists of "sufficient security for [an accused's] appearance" at trial, "he being supposed to continue in their friendly custody, instead of going to gaol."[3] Blackstone's reference to *sufficient security* presupposes property of some kind (money, of course, but something else of marketable value may suffice) that will be used to secure release. Because property is a key component of bail, class disparities have long informed legal practice, disparities that favor defendants with property over those without it.

The Constitution's Eighth Amendment, adopted in 1791, relies on this property-based approach to pretrial release. In most American jurisdictions, cash-up-front has been used as a device to ensure appearance at trial when addressing the two questions essential to release—(i) whether a defendant might flee and (ii) whether the public might be endangered by pretrial release.

In a data-driven legal system, algorithms offer a way to assess risks (i) and (ii). The fairness of the algorithms employed in today's system has been called into question, and we will turn to this shortly. We should note first, though, that, as applied to misdemeanor defendants, cash bail, when calculated according to currently available algorithms, appears not only to disadvantage the poor given the predictive criteria employed (a question of fairness, of course) but also to generate counterproductive results as far case outcomes are concerned. Research conducted in Houston during the mid-2010s confirms this point. In examining a large sample of similarly situated misdemeanor defendants in the Harris County court system (the system for Houston and surrounding localities), Paul Heaton and his colleagues found that, in the month following the day on which cash bail was set, defendants who posted bail had a lower rate of rearrest than those who didn't post it. After 30 days passed, however, the reverse proved to be the case. "[B]y one month after the [bail] hearing," Heaton discovered, "the average number of charges for detainees ... exceeded that of their similarly situated counterparts who were released."[4]

On this reckoning, cash bail isn't merely *un*productive, it's *counter*productive. "Detention increases the rate of guilty pleas and leads defendants to commit more crime in the future," Heaton writes. "On the basis of the rate of detention among people with $500 bail set," he states, Harris County would have released about 40,000 defendants pretrial during the period studied and "[t]hese individuals would have avoided approximately 5900 criminal convictions, many of which would have come through possibly erroneous guilty pleas." Clearly, there is a *criminal justice* benefit here, for it's never a good thing to induce someone to plead guilty to a crime he/she didn't come. And clearly, there's a *social justice* benefit, for the poor make up the great majority of those who fail to post cash bail. Over and above this, though, there's a *financial* benefit for government (and thus for the public at large). "On net, after accounting for both reductions in jail time and increases in population time," Heaton estimates, "the county would have saved an estimated $20 million in supervision costs alone. Thus, with better pretrial detention policy, Harris County could save millions of dollars per year, increase public safety, and likely reduce public convictions."[5]

Win, win, win, in other words, as far as cash bail for misdemeanor defendants are concerned. This statistical point is far from trivial since misdemeanor cases constitute more than 75% of the total criminal cases considered by the courts—so if the points just made concerning Harris County are extended to the country at large, the annual savings would easily exceed $100 million annually.[6] What about felonies, though? And what about the unusual misdemeanor case (spousal assault, for instance) where the risk of further violence is readily apparent? The answer to this can't be to release every defendant on his/her recognizance. Some defendants actually do pose flight risks (category (i) in the discussion above). Others may endanger the public at large while awaiting trial (category (ii)). And for a few, both types of risks exist.

Even if these considerations are taken into account, though, it will nonetheless be sound to abolish cash bail altogether, a goal Illinois has recently set out to achieve. Cash bail operates as a form of wealth discrimination for any kind of offense, so it can justifiably be retained if and only if there is no other way to guard against each type of risk. The legislation passed in Illinois, known as the SAFE-T Act of 2022, offers a sensible, (largely) wealth-neutral way of doing so. Under the legislation, those charged with low-level offenses must receive a pretrial release hearing within seven days; those deemed a flight risk must receive a hearing within 60 days; and those deemed a danger to the community must receive one within 90 days. When presiding over these hearings, judges are encouraged to consider options that don't include confinement, including electronic monitoring (such as GPS and home monitoring). Confinement in jail remains an option, then, but it's an option of last resort—and it's an option considered without regard to wealth.[7]

And what criteria should judges consider when responding to an application for pretrial release? It's here that algorithms come into play—or, to qualify this point slightly, they come into play if judges are to avoid seat-of-the-pants determinations concerning (i) and (ii). Prima facie, it seems clear that algorithms based on statistics are preferable to judicial intuition. This is merely a preliminary point, however, for there are features of contemporary statistics that make them unacceptable in principle in some instances and suspect in others. Each objection should be considered separately in order to understand the problematic features of algorithmic risk predictors—and thus their proper use in resolving bail applications.

Consider first a principled objection to the use of immutable characteristics—i.e., race and gender—when predicting behavior. (Given transgenderism, the term *immutable* is clearly a misnomer, but as long as transgenderism remains rare, this adjective, which continues to be widely employed in social science research, can still be used here.) Accuracy is substantially enhanced when these characteristics are included in predictions; correspondingly, it's diminished when they're omitted. If accuracy alone is our aim, immutable characteristics must be considered. But, of course, appeals to race and gender have often been invoked to further social injustice—and, for this reason, they are deemed suspect factors in constitutional law. Does this mean they should never be considered, then? If they are disregarded, predictive algorithms may prove to be less accurate than seat-of-the-pants judgments (which, of course, typically rely on race and gender, though *sub silentio*). There is thus a sound reason to continue to employ these characteristics when using algorithms, although we should do so warily.

Now consider the flaws in data used to make bail predictions. These flaws are attributable, in a multitude of ways, to the race- and class-based biases associated with arrest. Given these flaws, arrest data should not be taken as an accurate reflection of the likelihood that someone will offend in the future, for there are many offenses that go unreported and also there are many reported offenses that do not eventuate in arrests. Given these problems, arrest data can be said to inflate the role of racial minorities and the poor in the commission of crime. If treated as a reliable source of information in constructing algorithms that predict bail risks, this data will have a distortive effect on the predictions produced.

Does this mean that algorithmically generated predictions should be discarded? Two answers are in order here. One is that, in their present form, algorithms are so deeply flawed (because they rely on immutable characteristics) that they may be counterproductive as far as social justice is concerned. But the second answer is that, with the alterations in the exercise of discretion by police and other officials that (it's to be hoped) will occur in the decades to come, the data available to decision-makers may eventually contribute to the production of increasingly reliable predictions. This second reason provides the foundation for the cautious conclusion that's warranted concerning current use of algorithms. Even today, we can say, algorithmic predictions are preferable to seat-of-the-pants judgments concerning flight risk and danger to others. They're preferable, though, not because they warrant contemporary confidence in their content but, instead, because that content can be tested over time, with the result that the data-based predictions employed by future generations are likely to be sounder than the ones employed today.

Assistance of Counsel

Although the Sixth Amendment states that "[i]n all criminal prosecutions, the accused ... shall enjoy the assistance of counsel for his defence," it doesn't say that *the government* must pay for the assistance rendered to a defendant. Not only is the text silent on this point, it's clear that the Constitution, as originally understood, was not believed to impose an obligation on the government along these lines. The Supreme Court affirmed this initial understanding when it remarked in the 1891 case of *Van Duzee v. United States* that "[t]here is ... no general obligation on the part of the government [to] retain counsel for defendants or prisoners."[8] Given this point, it's clear that an unmistakable disadvantage for poor defendants was built into the original Constitution.

Gideon broke with this understanding. An earlier case, *Powell v. Alabama*, decided in 1932, took a step in *Gideon's* direction by requiring assistance of counsel for defendants facing the prospect of execution.[9]

Gideon built on *Powell* by holding that no felony defendant may be punished without assistance of counsel. Later cases went further, so that as of now, the rule is that any defendant may be imprisoned or deported only if he/she has received assistance of counsel at the time of the initial adjudication of guilt—or has been given an opportunity to waive this right.

And what about defendants who face neither the possibility of imprisonment nor deportation? The answer to this is that the Court has not otherwise imposed an obligation to offer a lawyer (though aliens must be warned about the risk of deportation).[10] In particular, guilty pleas to misdemeanors that can't lead to imprisonment or deportation remain constitutionally acceptable. Because misdemeanor cases predominate in criminal law, and because many can't result in imprisonment (but may lead to a conviction that results in the loss of, say, a job or housing), a substantial percentage of current cases continue to be adjudicated in the absence of counsel. The poor, in other words, continue to be disadvantaged in criminal cases under the current Court's interpretation of the Constitution.

Two challenges to this legal framework might be advanced, one based on the text, the other on considerations of fair treatment. The textual challenge is straightforward. Because the Sixth Amendment speaks of "all criminal prosecutions," someone might argue, no criminal conviction can be deemed constitutionally acceptable unless counsel is provided—and the government therefore must provide a lawyer to any defendant unable to afford one if it is to impose constitutionally legitimate punishment. *All* doesn't mean *some*, a proponent of this textual challenge would note—indeed, it can't if the text merits respect. Admittedly, the original understanding was that *no* defendant is entitled to representation at government expense, the person advancing this argument would concede, but now that *Powell, Gideon*, and a host of later cases have required provision of counsel in certain circumstances, the only reasonable way to honor the text, an advocate of this position would maintain, is to say that *all* means all.

Is this too legalistic—too formalistic—a rationale for extending *Gideon*? Even if it's rejected on this ground, a different rationale, one that relies on considerations of social justice rather than textualism, points in the same direction. No point in the criminal process is more important to a defendant than the moment at which guilt is adjudicated, an advocate of this alternative approach would contend. If finances stand in the way of challenging the state's case, then the criminal law can of course be characterized as a system that favors the rich over the poor. It's a system that, indirectly, disadvantages Blacks and Hispanics since they are disproportionately poor, but it's also one that directly, and openly, advantages the prosperous over the impecunious, whatever their race absent a rule that provides lawyers for defendants in all cases. "[R]eason and reflection require us to recognize that in our adversary system of criminal justice," the Court remarked in *Gideon*, "any person who is haled into court, who is too poor to hire a lawyer, cannot be assured a fair trial unless counsel is provided for him."[11] In making this point, *Gideon* embraced a general principle of justice. As applied, that principle was limited to felony trials. Clearly, though, it's pertinent across the board—to all punitive deprivations of liberty by the government—and because it is, it links considerations of social justice to criminal justice. On this reckoning, *all* must mean all, not merely as a matter of textual analysis, but also because no other application of the principle stated in *Gideon* ensures the integration of social justice and criminal justice.

In implementing this principle, we should consider three issues: first, assistance of counsel claims in settings purportedly guaranteed under current law but nonetheless sometimes not honored in practice; second, assistance claims that aren't recognized through current interpretation of the Constitution but that must be if *all* is to mean all; and third, collateral matters related to assistance of counsel, in particular the proper measure to use when thinking about the scope of service indigent defendants should be provided by comparison with prosperous ones.

As for the first issue, although the Court now requires provision of counsel in any case that eventuates in imprisonment or deportation, it's clear that some jurisdictions don't honor this rule. This is clear for a simple reason—because some states fail to allocate enough funds for indigent defendants. For example, in the wake of the Court's ruling in the 2002 case of *Alabama v. Shelton*, which held that defendants faced with the prospect of incarceration following probation revocation must be afforded counsel when guilt is adjudicated,[12] the Chief Justice of South Carolina denounced the decision as "misguided." "If we adhered to it in South Carolina," the chief Justice continued,

> we would have the right to counsel probably … by dragooning lawyers out of their offices in every magistrate's court in South Carolina, and I have simply told my magistrates that we just don't have the resources to do

> that. So I will tell you straight up that we [are] not adhering to *Alabama v. Shelton* in every situation.[13]

Financial limits prevent implementation of constitutional rights, then—limitations that might be overcome if the legislature were to move money from matters that are not subject to constitutional protection. Alongside this is a gray area of non-compliance, one in which jurisdictions appear to honor the law but, in all likelihood, fail to do so. This gray area has to do with the fees charged by public defenders' offices—i.e., with the payments defendants must make to secure representation. The Court has held that if an indigent defendant is entitled to representation under its interpretation of the Constitution, a trial court may not treat that defendant's failure to pay a public defender's fees as an automatic reason to impose punishment.[14] It's by no means clear, though, that all courts provide this information to indigent defendants. In any event, some courts use civil contempt orders to pressure indigent defendants, thus creating a kind of debtors' prison within the legal system.[15]

Beyond this are issues that implicate *Gideon* indirectly. Foremost among the latter are *Miranda* warnings. *Miranda* is a critically important feature of the legal landscape, in part because of its *Gideon*-inspired warning to each suspect that if he/she can't afford an attorney the state will provide one. Of even more importance for our purposes is *Miranda's* effect in providing a suspect with an incentive not to accept responsibility for his/her acts, for whenever a criminal defense lawyer urges a client to withhold a confession to maximize its strategic value, the effect of this act of withholding is also to reduce the likelihood of taking responsibility for wrongdoing. Michelle Alexander doesn't mention this point when discussing restorative justice.[16] Nonetheless, it's clear that the restorative justice reconciliation process can unfold only when a suspect is willing to waive the *Miranda* right—or to put this point in an international context, the restorative justice process may never reach the point of victim-offender reconciliation *in any of the world's major legal systems* since most of them have a *Miranda*-type requirement of a knowing waiver of the right against self-incrimination.[17]

To note this isn't to deprecate either the emphasis on accountability essential to restorative justice or the values associated with *Miranda*, for each contributes to social justice. *But they contribute in different, and potentially incompatible, ways.* Because *Miranda* furthers social justice considerations (by warning indigent defendants of the right to remain silent and also of the right to an attorney), someone seeking to integrate these considerations into the administration of criminal law must accept the possibility of tension between, on the one hand, its inclusion of lawyers in the criminal process and, on the other hand, reliance on a restorative justice process. Resolution of the tension is possible by means of a compromise: a defendant can waive the *Miranda* right (and so take responsibility for harm done) on condition that the court accept his/her guilty plea—and can otherwise retract the waiver.[18] This of course is not the *un*conditional acceptance of responsibility typically associated with someone's acknowledgment of accountability. The compromise just outlined does, however, resolve an otherwise irresolvable tension between *Miranda* and the restorative justice process.

A further factor, one that will add complexity to inquiries into personal accountability only if the Constitution is interpreted to include a social justice consideration not currently attributed to it, should be considered. At present, indigent defendants who claim that a mental disease or defect undermined their capacity to conform to the law are not granted psychiatric aid of their own when preparing a defense. Rather, they must share the services of a psychiatrist, a psychiatrist who will submit an expert opinion in favor of one side or the other.[19] Clearly, this is inadequate as a matter of basic justice. Prosperous defendants routinely hire psychiatrists to mount their own defenses; as a matter of comparative justice, indigent defendants must be able to do so as well. Furthermore, because people with mental health disorders are disproportionately present among those charged with, and convicted of, crimes, it's particularly urgent for criminal defendants not merely to receive diagnoses from experts who are appointed to care for them but also to receive ongoing therapeutic counseling to address their problems.

This is an argument that can be advanced without considering the accountability process. Only a moment's thought is needed, though, to realize that it has ramifications for those called on to account for their acts. This is because a valid claim of a mental health disorder can undermine an ascription of responsibility for harming others. Needless to say, there's room for disagreement as to the validity of such claims. But given the number of inmates who are believed to suffer from mental disorders,[20] it's essential to inquire into this possibility. Moreover, given a social justice perspective, one must consider the hypothesis that public institutions—schools, for instance, and the health care system—often fail to diagnose mental health disorders at an early stage, with the result that behavioral problems that might have been contained in adolescence become problems for the criminal law at a later stage. It may still be possible to reconcile this point in a given case with someone's acceptance of personal accountability. The road to this conclusion may turn out to be a winding one, however.

And what about the third issue mentioned above—the quality of representation offered to indigent defendants? In the years following *Gideon*, the Court held that, whenever a defendant is entitled to representation, *assistance of counsel* means not only that counsel will be provided an indigent person but also that *effective* counsel will be provided. Of course, *effective* is a word with less than clear boundaries. Well-off defendants call on a wide array of services. They not only can draw on the collateral services just mentioned (psychiatric experts of their own choosing, etc.), they also sometimes draw on more than one lawyer to advance their claims. If the most prosperous defendants are taken as the measure for determining what constitutes *effective assistance of counsel*, then, the cost to the public could be astronomic.

Similar problems of scope arise when other services are provided at taxpayer expense. The standard for determining per-pupil expenditures in public education might be calculated by considering practices at elite private schools, for instance—and the standard for determining medical expenses available to any member of the public might be calculated by considering reimbursement practices for patients with ambitious insurance plans. Just as these options have not served as the measure for determining the scope of taxpayer obligations in education and medicine, it would also be inappropriate to use the level of expenditure of rich criminal defendants in trying to determine the scope of *effective assistance of counsel*. The Court thus hasn't taken this route. Unfortunately, though, the approach it actually has adopted makes it possible for the indigent to receive far less attention than is needed in numerous settings. This is because the Court has stated that it presumes effective counsel is provided whenever a licensed lawyer is provided an indigent defendant.[21] In taking this position, the Court has placed the burden on an indigent defendant to demonstrate that this presumption hasn't been satisfied in any given criminal setting. And because that burden has to be satisfied *after* a guilty verdict has been reached, it's extremely difficult to meet the standard in practice.

It's particularly unfortunate that this is the framework employed for measuring effectiveness, for there is an obvious alternative available here. In adopting this other approach, a court reviewing effectiveness claims would ask whether a jurisdiction is spending approximately the same amount per case on criminal defense services as it spends on the prosecution of indigent defendants. If it does, the presumption just mentioned should be adopted. But if the jurisdiction fails to maintain rough parity between the two sides, there is no need to consider the difficult questions associated with the presumption, for then it's clear that the legal system is organized in a way that disadvantages the poor. To put this point differently, we can say that *Gideon's* principle is violated if substantially more funds are spent on prosecuting the poor. Parity is essential as a matter of social justice in this context.

Notes

1. *Gideon v. Wainwright*, 372 U.S. 335 (1963).
2. "... nor shall excessive bail be imposed ..." U.S. Constitution, Amendment 8.
3. William Blackstone, *Commentaries on the Laws of England* 4: 293–94 (1769).
4. Paul Heaton et al., "The Downstream Consequences of Misdemeanor Trial Detention," *Stanford Law Review* 69: 711, 761 (2017).
5. Id. 768.
6. See Sandra Mayson and Megan Stevenson, "Misdemeanors by the Numbers," *B.C.L. Rev.* 61: 971 (2020).
7. For an overview of the act, see ICJIA, "Roles and Responsibilities under the 2021 Safe T Act" @icjia.illinois.gov/about/publications/the-2021-safe-t-act-icjia-roles-and-responsibilities.
8. *United States v. Van Duzee*, 140 U.S. 169, 173 (1891).
9. *Powell v. Alabama*, 287 U.S. 45 (1932).
10. See *Padilla v. Kentucky*, 559 U.S. 356 (2010).
11. 372 U.S. at 344.
12. *Alabama v. Shelton*, 535 U.S. 564 (2002).
13. As quoted in Alexandra Natapoff, *Punishment without Crime* 79 (2018).
14. See *Bearden v. Georgia*, 461 U.S. 660 (1983).
15. See Natapoff, *supra* note 13 at 140.

16. When Alexander talks about her sample of participants in the restorative justice process, her reference to "the people who choose to participate" appears to be limited to victims and their families. Alexander, *supra* note 16 in Chapter 3. However, there must be another group that chooses to participate, for criminal defendants must be willing to waive their *Miranda* rights if they are to engage in the apologetic reconciliation essential to the culmination of restorative justice.
17. In a survey of international practice conducted by researchers for the Library of Congress, the authors note: "[t]he warnings jurisdictions vary, but typically include the right to remain silent and the right to legal counsel." Law Library of Congress Legal Research Center, *Miranda Warning Equivalents Abroad* 1 (2016).
18. American Bar Association, *Victim-Offender Mediation/Dialogue Program Requirements* (April 1994) @americanbar.org/content/dam/aba/directories/policy/annual-1994/1994_am_101b.pdf.
19. See *Ake v Oklahoma*, 470 U.S. 68 (1985) and *McWilliams inv. Dunn*, 582 U.S. 183 (2017).
20. For a summary of research findings that have established the disproportionate presence of inmates (by comparison with the population at large) who suffer from mental health disorders, see Prison Policy initiative, *Mental Health* (2023), at prisonpolicy.org/research/mental_health.
21. See, e.g., *Strickland v. Washington*, 466 U.S. 668 (1984).

CHAPTER 7

Sentencing: Surveying Current Practices

Sentencing is the culmination of the criminal process. The sentence imposed need not involve punishment; it most certainly need not involve incarceration. On the contrary, given the expansion of options for sentencers in the modern era (community service is a quasi-punitive outcome, for instance; electronic surveillance is punitive but avoids incarceration), a wide variety of possibilities exists. Because one of the book's aims is to identify steps that will reduce mass incarceration (and so to introduce a social justice consideration into a pressing issue of the day), it takes an approach to sentencing that relies on penal parsimony, an approach that doesn't advocate prison abolition but that nonetheless seeks to reduce the scope of punishment and that reduces state reliance on imprisonment.

Earlier chapters have laid the foundation for this. Chapters 3 and 4 discussed the accountability inquiry that's essential to the criminal process. They also provided a rationale for adopting a culpability scale that will promote uniformity in sentencing, a scale based on presumptions rather than mandated outcomes, but, nonetheless, a framework of sufficient strength as to reduce the risk that, say, rape will often be punished more severely than murder. The previous chapter noted how a defendant's exercise of the *Miranda* right can make it less likely that the defendant will acknowledge responsibility for his/her acts. It also noted how a much-needed enlargement of the scope of mental health services,

W. C. Heffernan, *Social Justice/Criminal Justice*,
https://doi.org/10.1007/978-3-031-75397-8_7

while desirable from the standpoint of social justice, might have a similar effect. Subsequent chapters comment further on accountability issues. The final chapter deals with mass incarceration: it discusses social justice investments that can reduce the likelihood of crime and it elaborates on the penal parsimony principle, which will reduce the state's reliance on incarceration.

This chapter deals with preliminary issues in sentencing, and in doing so it introduces the possibility of less punitive sentences in the context of the current problematic legal regime. Its opening section examines the significance of the distinction between comparative and non-comparative justice as this is applied to criminal sentencing. The chapter's second section deals with public and private features of sentencing, in particular the behind-closed-doors bargaining between prosecutors and criminal defense lawyers. Neither section takes a stand as to how sentencing ought to be conducted; indeed, given the fact that the criminal process, as currently administered, is managed mostly through prosecution/defense lawyer negotiation in the shadow of sentencing standards set by a legislature, the process stands out for its relative indifference to the act of taking personal responsibility that should be central to a decent society's legal system.

The chapter's final two sections examine sentencing outcomes in the current legal system. These are discussed in the context of modest reform, reform that accepts the current organization of sentencing but that argues for the most lenient outcomes (across the board) now produced. The chapters in the following section of the book imagine the more fundamental systemic change that would occur with a pervasive commitment to social justice beyond the legal system. Here, we focus on change within the system.

Sentencing: Comparative Justice and Non-Comparative Justice Perspectives

It's not only possible—it's actually common—to bring non-comparative and also comparative justice perspectives to bear on sentencing.[1] At the outset, think for a moment about the distinction's relevance to grading student papers. *It's an A paper*, a student might say in making a non-comparative justice complaint about a grade of *B*, a complaint that implies the following—whatever the grades other students may have received for the assignment, *this* paper merited an *A* because it satisfies the conditions (not necessarily specified when the complaint is made but readily supplied if requested) of a first-rate writing assignment.

More complicated arguments are needed to support comparative justice claims. At a minimum, a student receiving a *B* would need to know the range and frequency of all grades awarded for a given assignment to make a plausible argument. Standing alone, though, this claim would still be weak. This is because someone might ask about the grades awarded for comparable paper submissions for the assignment. It's possible, after all, that the person awarding grades wasn't an "easy *A*," in which case the student complaining of comparative injustice might have a compelling objection to a grade awarded to the same paper if submitted in a different section of the course but wouldn't have a valid complaint concerning his/her paper grade from the professor—or, in reframing this argument, the complainant would have to explain why student grades in another section should be considered relevant to a claim of comparative justice.

Once these points are taken into account, one can readily understand why people tend to use the rhetoric of non-comparative justice when considering evaluative institutional practices, for comparative justice claims aren't merely fact-specific, they also rely on comparisons of the assessments made of ***similarly situated*** parties. As it happens, the kind of detailed information needed to make credible comparative justice claims about institutional outcomes (about college admissions, hiring by corporations, for instance—and sentencing) has become available in the modern era. It's accessible through datasets and tables, not through seat-of-the-pants judgments about institutional fairness. We had an opportunity to consider a claim of comparative injustice in Chapter 5, where Table 1 revealed a pattern of different "hit rates" of similarly situated motorists from different ethnic groups. Because the motorists stopped by the police were similar in relevant respects to one another, there was reason to believe that ethnic background played a role in triggering the police decision to intervene.

Data examined in this chapter will also be analyzed from a comparative justice perspective. As will be seen, there is an inconclusiveness to comparative justice reasoning, for even when it can be shown that two groups are similarly situated and that group *A* is treated more harshly than *B*, the question arises whether to *level up* (enhance the harshness for *B*) or *level down* (reduce the harshness for *A*). This issue can be resolved only by considering the empirical findings concerning differential treatment while stepping outside those findings to make an evaluative judgment about the proper approach to the entire practice under consideration. As far as sentencing is concerned, the overall perspective that will be employed will be informed by a preference for lenity, a preference that points toward downward revisions of sentences to the lowest levels of current practice (while reasoning within the confines of the current system) and that points toward adoption of the penal parsimony principle (while engaging in across the board revision of the current sentencing process).

After commenting at some length on comparative justice, a word is in order about its non-comparative counterpart. At first, this approach may see crude, perhaps even naïve, since it disregards data about everyday practice in favor of flat-out, yes/no judgments of social life. Only a moment's thought is needed, however, to establish that this perspective is widely entertained—arguably, even more widely entertained than the comparative one. It's entertained as a reserve position on justice—as the source of judgments few people seem the need to examine but that define the range of the acceptable and unacceptable for most human activity. As far as punishment is concerned, for instance, the non-comparative perspective is widely thought to settle questions about the unacceptability of certain practices. Sanguinary punishments such as whipping and ear-cropping—to take obvious examples—are off the table. There's no need to ask about the frequency and range of their administration, no need to consider their impact on different portions of the population. Rather, they're per se unacceptable, even if administered once. Generalize on this to the thousands of punishments that might be (but aren't) deployed and one can grasp the potential scope of non-comparative reasoning.

Pronouncing a Sentence in Open Court, Bargaining Behind Closed Doors

One other general point about sentencing should be considered before turning to statistics about current practice, a point that's understandable in terms of the contrast between public accessibility and secrecy in making sentencing decisions. This is that criminal charges, whether contained in an indictment or an information, are announced to the public, as is the disposition of those charges, but that the charges themselves are typically resolved in private, during secret conversations involving three experts (the judge, the prosecutor, and the defense attorney), though the conversations often involve only the latter two. The conversations are secret because the parties are bargaining, and bargains involve give-and-take—that is, in bargaining, parties often adopt and relinquish positions they later regret, something that's facilitated by a promise of confidentiality among everyone involved.

And what's subject to bargaining here? The answer to this is that virtually every feature of a case may be bargained over: charge bargaining may occur prior to an indictment or information, but if no charges are bargained over (i.e., if a defendant's lawyer has nothing to do with the creation of an indictment) plea and sentence bargaining remain possible. Indeed, of the three issues just mentioned (and others might be deemed relevant in any given context), sentence bargaining is likely to be particularly intense, for it's the outcome of the criminal process—the punishment imposed—likeliest to motivate an offender.

Charge-, plea-, and sentencing-bargaining pervade the criminal process. (The term *plea bargaining* will henceforth be used to refer to all of them.) At present, about 90% of criminal cases culminate in bargains between defendants and prosecutors.[2] The court system would have a hard time functioning if that figure were to fall to, say, 50%. Most criminal defense lawyers are aware of this. The threat of system-overload is one of the two most important bargaining chips available to them in their dealings with prosecutors, the other being the possibility of their clients refusing to waive the *Miranda* right. As against this, prosecutors are armed by the legislature with statutes that impose penalties heavier than those in other advanced industrialized societies for similar crimes; charging discretion to seek consecutive, as distinguished from concurrent, terms (as when a defendant refuses to waive the *Miranda* right); and, when appropriate, mandatory minima suited to a defendant's criminal history.

Prosecutors and criminal defense lawyers view these as tradeable resources. The outcome is a confession offered in exchange for leniency. Only an unperceptive defendant would fail to note the transactional basis of the entire process. In standing before a judge and delivering a carefully rehearsed confession of guilt followed by a pre-arranged sentence imposed in open court, a defendant is likely to realize that it was the product of a bargain—that an admission of guilt was the price to be paid for the prosecutor's exercise of charging restraint.

In many criminal proceedings, the victim encounters the defendant only at this moment of pre-arranged confession. The victim has been given many opportunities to speak prior to this, but none (in light of the defense lawyer's concern about *Miranda* in a setting where the victim can seek an apology) occurs when the offender is present, for if the victim were to address the offender, this might provoke a confession. To lessen the tension between *Miranda* and restorative justice, one might permit conditional plea negotiations—that is, a jurisdiction might adopt a rule that makes a defendant's statement during negotiations inadmissible at trial unless the defendant agrees to plead guilty to a charge based on that statement. Admittedly, conditionality of this kind makes clear the transactional nature of plea negotiations.[3] It can be defended, however, on the ground that it effects a compromise between *Miranda* and restorative justice. Ideally, someone should take *un*conditional responsibility for his/her acts. But given *Miranda* (and given the important social justice considerations associated with its warnings), this compromise is preferable to insistence on either one to the exclusion of the other.

To focus solely on *Miranda*, though, is to disregard other troubling features of the plea bargaining process—the decisive role of experts in settling on a sentence (and thus, the non-participation of jurors/laypeople in the resolution of most criminal cases), the view of the law as a set of bargaining chips available to both parties, the draconian penalties often available to the prosecutor, and the overall impression that an admission of guilt is the product of a transactional relationship, not an expression of genuine remorse. These defects are so substantial as to warrant rethinking current sentencing practices from the ground up. The data on sentencing in the remainder of the chapter—data on non-capital crimes in the next sub-section, and data on capital crimes in the subsequent one—are thus not provided as part of an effort to reform current practice fundamentally. Such practice is too deeply compromised to be subject to far-reaching modification. Rather, the road to serious change will be outlined in the three chapters contained in Section IV, which presupposes public agreement on the need to design a decent society (and thus to de-emphasize punishment while focusing on accountability to those harmed). This chapter will, however, adhere to the *within* premise that's informed commentary throughout Section III. It will adopt a *level down* approach to disparities, an approach that might lead to modest results. Generalized ambitiously (and adopted in a decent society), the *level down* direction advocated in this chapter will substantially reduce mass incarceration. This, however, is likely only when there is a society-wide commitment to modifying the operation of the criminal law—a subject for Section IV.

Non-Capital Sentencing

Stories abound about the legal system's favored treatment of socially privileged defendants. In 2015, for instance, Brock Turner, a member of the Stanford University swimming team, was spotted by two bicyclists at 1 a.m. near campus while he was on top of a young lady whose undergarments had been ripped off. According to one of the cyclists, Turner attempted to flee when questioned about what he was doing. The cyclists prevented his escape, and the young lady later stated that she'd passed out at the time Turner assaulted her. Charged with sexual assault and rape, the prosecution sought a sentence of six years imprisonment. Turner was sentenced to only six months, and served three months that were followed by a term of probation. The judge who imposed this sentence was criticized for it and eventually was denied reappointment, but the sentence itself wasn't modified.[4]

In another case, Robert Richards, a great-grandson of the founder of the DuPont Corporation, received probation and an eight-year suspended sentence after admitting that he had raped his three-year daughter. Richards was more than six feet tall and weighed over 250 pounds at the time of the sentencing. Nonetheless, the judge who settled on the sentence stated that Richards "would not fare well in prison" and thus should not serve time there.[5]

Clearly, Richards's sentence and Turner's cry out for counterfactuals—that is, they call out for evidence of how defendants from disadvantaged backgrounds but charged with similar crimes would have fared in the legal system. Lacking data on this, we can only assume that they received sentencing breaks *because of* their social advantages. Unfortunately, we can't say more with any confidence about either counterfactual possibility, for while there is substantial data concerning similarly situated defendants as far as race and gender are concerned in non-capital cases, there is none concerning wealth. We're thus left with anecdotes—anecdotes (like the two just mentioned) that suggest the strong possibility that class advantages can be exploited either at the charging or sentencing stages of the criminal process but that can't be considered sufficient in themselves to establish this as a clear-cut feature of the criminal law.

We thus should turn to race and gender. Here, data maintained by the United States Sentencing Commission (USSC) provide incontrovertible evidence of disparate outcomes in similarly situated non-capital cases. Standing alone, though, the data don't substantiate a conclusion of *unjustified* disparities, for different racial or gender outcomes may be attributable to culpability considerations that don't register in the statistics provided by the USSC. Nonetheless, given what we know, one can still use the term *troubling* to characterize long-standing patterns in federal sentencing.

To understand why the differences are troubling, it's necessary to step back and understand the mechanics of sentencing in federal courts. Concerned about the broad discretion federal judges were exercising when settling on sentences, Congress adopted a statutory framework of determinate sentencing during the 1980s, one that required judges to use an offender score (computed by reference to the offence charged plus consideration of a defendant's criminal history) when imposing punishment within a specified sentencing range. Under this scheme, a sentence could exceed or fall below the prescribed range only if a judge provided a specific reason for doing so. The legislation thus established a *presumptive sentencing* framework, one that would constrain judicial discretion (and thus focus attention primarily on culpability) in most cases but that would allow for occasional exceptions once these could be justified in unusual circumstances.[6]

In *Booker v. United States*, decided in 2005, the Supreme Court modified, but didn't entirely set aside, this legislative framework. At stake in *Booker* was a claim that it is unconstitutional for a sentencing judge to consider information neither admitted by a defendant nor proved to a jury beyond a reasonable doubt. The Court agreed with this argument. Rather than reject the entire framework adopted two decades earlier, though, it held that the guidelines essential to the legislation should be treated as advisory rather than mandatory. The sentencing framework adopted two decades earlier thus survived *Booker*, but it did so only through a constitutional ruling that enhanced judicial discretion, a ruling that opened the door to the risk of bias in responding to factors unrelated to culpability.[7]

As is shown in Table 2 (see Appendix), USSC data establish that guidelines departures actually did increase in the post-*Booker* era. Scholarly research hasn't conclusively demonstrated that these departures have exacerbated racial and gender sentencing disparities. The 2023 USSC report contains the following summary. For the period 2016–23, it states, "Black males received sentences 13.4 percent longer, and Hispanic males 11.4 percent longer, than White males."[8] It's essential to emphasize continuity here: double-digit racial disparities have existed throughout the last two decades. During the 20-year period preceding the 2023 report—i.e., before and after Booker—Black male offenders received sentences longer than their White peers (19.1% longer from 2012 to 2016, and roughly similar in earlier times).

Racial disparities were particularly clear as far as probation is concerned. "Black males were 23.4 percent less likely, and Hispanic males 26.6 percent less likely, to receive a probationary sentence compared to White males," the report states. In particular, the report notes, "Black male offenders were 21.2 percent less likely [than White male offenders] to receive a non-government sponsored downward departure or variance" in the years following 2012—that is, Black males were about one-fifth less likely than their White male counterparts to receive a reduction in time as a result of a factor not mentioned in the sentencing guidelines but considered pertinent to reduction in incarceration by judges imposing a sentence.[9]

As shown in Table 2, average prison sentences for Black male offenders were 50% higher than for White male offenders at the beginning of the twenty-first century. In the last ten years, however, the gap has steadily closed, and by 2020 it had disappeared. For female offenders, the gap has not only closed but reversed: average sentences for White females have been substantially longer than those for Black or Hispanic females for the last decade, and the gap has been growing in recent years. Criminologists have yet to fully explain this puzzling development. Michael Light highlights policy shifts at the Department of Justice and the move away from the use of mandatory minimum sentences in drug cases,[10] while Mona Lynch et al. suggest that judicial discretion may have countered the return to a more punitive stance at the DOJ since 2017.[11]

We're left, then, with a mystery that has yet to be comprehensively explained. On the one hand, because Black and Hispanic defendants continue to receive longer sentences than similarly situated Whites (particularly with respect to probation), it might be said that federal courts have relied on a standard racialized and gendered stereotype about criminality. On this stereotype, Black males are particularly blameworthy for their acts, White males less so, and Black females even less so. It's possible that granular analysis of the data might provide support for this stereotype. It's also possible, though, that prosecutors (in particular) have altered their focus, marking White offenders as a particular object of concern.

Nonetheless, despite this recent trend, the long-standing and persistent one can't be ignored: that discretion exercised by federal officials (even before *Booker* and perhaps even more so afterwards) is guided by implicit biases, biases that favor women over men and that, among men, favor Whites over Blacks. The points made here don't conclusively establish the soundness of this implicit bias hypothesis, it should be emphasized. They're compatible with it, however, given the persistence of the patterns at stake.

Because of their compatibility, the points made so far suggest a remedy for addressing racial and gender disparities, one in which a *leveling down* direction should be adopted rather than one that *levels up*. Unfortunately, as we've just seen, sentences for White male defendants are *leveling up*, moving toward the already-elevated levels for Black males. This isn't to say that the direction of change will always be toward more punishment; even in the current problematic social context, there has been a modest decline in overall incarceration levels. It is, however, to suggest that the prospects for a substantial, across the board *level down*—one that exceeds the current rates for Black females—are remote. For this, a commitment to a decent society, one that views criminal justice in the context of social justice, will be needed. In the meantime, *level down* (by taking the sentences imposed on Black females as a guide to reform within the current system).

Capital Sentencing

There are important differences between capital and non-capital sentencing. Nonetheless, sentencing in capital cases is as compromised as it is in its non-capital counterpart. Some of the reasons for this have to do with institutional structure, some with the peculiar type of racial disparities associated with administration of the death penalty. These differences are sufficiently significant as to make it worthwhile to consider capital sentencing on its own.

Consider procedural issues first. Although most advanced industrialized societies abolished capital punishment during the second half of the twentieth century, a substantial percentage of American states retained it. In *Gregg v. Georgia*, decided in 1976, the Supreme Court placed limits on the way in which the death penalty may be administered. The *Gregg* Court was concerned with the same general issue examined in the previous sub-section of this chapter—the possibility that sentencing discretion may be exercised in a biased way. *Gregg*, however, did not employ the guidelines framework used in non-capital cases. Rather, it adopted a bifurcated approach for capital trials. A jury in a capital case must first consider questions about a defendant's guilt, *Gregg* held. Only if it finds a defendant guilty of a capital offense, *Gregg* further held, will the jury consider the question of whether to impose a sentence of death. If it settles on execution, the jury must make an affirmative determination that an aggravating circumstance (murdering a police officer, for instance) is present—*and* even if such a finding is made, *Gregg* further held, the jury must remain free to decide that any mitigating circumstance it may deem relevant to the case overrides its finding of an aggravating circumstance.[12]

As in non-capital sentencing, then, the *Gregg* framework aims at channeling sentencing discretion. It does so in a different way, though; in particular, it does so by requiring a specific finding of extra culpability with respect to a capital crime (i.e., an aggravating circumstance) while permitting sentences to set this finding aside on determining that it's overridden by a mitigating circumstance. The *Gregg* framework presupposes active lay participation (i.e., juror) in capital sentencing, then. In this respect, it differs from non-capital sentencing, which, in practice, is the product of closed-door decision-making. But *Gregg* promotes lay participation to confer constitutional legitimacy on the most drastic of all punishments, the execution of a human being.

Have verdicts rendered in the last half-century at least had the effect of reducing unjustified racial disparities? In 1976, at the time *Gregg* was decided, the steepest disparities were associated with rape rather than murder.[13] Rape is no longer an issue in death penalty litigation. This is because the Supreme Court prohibited execution for rape in the years following *Gregg*. An across-the-board prohibition of this kind relies on a rationale of non-comparative justice: it holds that under no possible circumstances (even the most heinous ones imaginable) may someone who commits rape without committing homicide be executed for this. We will return to this non-comparative justice approach to punishment in a later chapter. What matters here are two different claims—first, that racial disparities in the administration of the death penalty need only be considered with respect to homicide and second, that an argument based on non-comparative justice can *also* be advanced against the death penalty.

Numerous studies have examined the racial disparity issue at stake in capital sentencing. The leading one was undertaken by David Baldus, a sociologist and law professor who concentrated on capital sentencing in Georgia. (Later studies have examined other states, each located in the south, since this is where the death penalty is most frequently administered, but because these studies have reached conclusions consistent in most respects with those reached by Baldus, we should focus on his results). Baldus's approach is best understood in terms of the culpability concerns that prompted the *Gregg* Court to adopt its bifurcated approach to sentencing. A sentence of death is unbiased under *Gregg*, Baldus assumed, if it's based on the aggravating circumstances present in a given case. One race may be sentenced to death at a higher rate than another, in other words, but this disparity can be justified as long as attention is given to aggravating circumstances.

In surveying data from Georgia's actual administration of the death penalty, Baldus found partial confirmation for the culpability hypothesis. That is, he established that in the absence of aggravating circumstances, the death penalty was imposed with few racial disparities. He did not find this when aggravating circumstances were present, though. On the contrary, in examining four types of cases (White-on-White homicides, White-on-Black homicides, Black-on-Black homicides, and Black-on-Black homicides), he found significant disparities as to the race of victims *that could not be explained by culpability considerations.* Homicides involving a White victim (whether committed by a White or a Black defendant) produced a higher rate of death sentences than homicides involving a Black victim (again, whether committed by a White or a Black victim) even when controlling for culpability considerations. This point held true both for prosecutorial charging decisions and jury sentencing, Baldus found. That is, Georgia prosecutors brought death penalty charges, and Georgia juries sentenced defendants to death, more frequently in White-victim cases than in Black-victim cases—and they did so in ways that could not be explained by reference to the aggravating circumstances framework essential to *Gregg*. In summarizing his results, Baldus remarked, it is "highly plausible that the statistically significant race-of-victim effects documented in the literature reflect a devaluing (conscious or unconscious) of black murder victims."[14]

There is, of course, an ironic side to this finding, for (given the fact that intraracial homicides are more common than interracial ones) the pattern Baldus identified means that Black homicide defendants are *less* likely to be sentenced to death, given similar levels of culpability, than White homicide defendants. This irony of capital punishment is inextricably linked to a point about its arbitrariness, though, for the Baldus conclusion also establishes that the death penalty is imposed in a way that downplays culpability in favor of a deeply troubling feature of everyday life, one that accords greater value to White over Black lives. (Indeed, Table 3 provides double confirmation of the Baldus hypothesis: more severe punishment for Blacks convicted of homicide at the end of Jim Crow (1930–1960) and less severe punishment today as contemporary sentencing juries have disproportionately saved the lives of Black capital defendants charged with killing Black victims. In both the past and the present, then, Black lives have been accorded lesser value, though for different reasons.)

We encountered a similar pattern in the third chapter, where we saw that in her 1939 study of the administration of criminal law in Mississippi, Hortense Powdermaker observed that "[w]hen a white man kills a Negro, it is hardly considered murder"—and, further, as Powdermaker also noted, Black-on-Black homicides were taken less seriously than their White-on-White analogues. Conducting research in the deep south two generations later, Baldus encountered the same pattern of racial devaluation Powdermaker had identified.[15] Baldus, of course, was able to introduce statistical tools Powdermaker didn't employ. But the pattern remained the same: state power was deployed both in the early and late twentieth century to affirm the lesser dignity of Blacks as opposed to Whites. Table 3 confirms this point about the vestiges of Jim Crow through its analysis of modern data bearing on the death penalty in North Carolina. Furthermore, by focusing on North Carolina, Table 3 shows that the racial patterns Baldus found in Georgia's contemporary administration to the death penalty are not confined to that state.

And what about non-comparative justice? To those opposed to the death penalty in all circumstances, the issue here has to do with the intrinsic wrongfulness of an intentional killing of a human being when the person killed poses no imminent threat to the life of another. A person adopting this rationale must be prepared to defend it in any conceivable context—must be prepared to defend it against obvious counterexamples, and so must reject the possibility of executing paradigmatically evil mass murderers such as Hitler, Pol Pot, and Idi Amin. *Even* these people are immune from execution under the principle just outlined, its proponent would contend. The principle may seem simple-minded, but non-comparative reasoning focuses on clear principle, not on inconclusive comparisons of discrimination against members of one group or another.

If we return to questions about the inconclusiveness of comparative justice approaches to the Baldus findings, we can see that these approaches don't offer a way to arbitrate between *level up* and *level down*.

Even-handed administration of the death penalty would be promoted by executing more defendants who have killed White victims (*leveling up*), though it might also be made even-handed by executing fewer defendants who have killed Black defendants (*leveling down*). Because comparative justice provides no conclusive way to choose between these options and because the non-comparative rationale against the death penalty amounts to a bald assertion (that many reject), it has to be granted that, despite differences in reasons, the administration of capital punishment, as currently practiced, is subject to serious challenge.

If, on the other hand, we introduce a preference-for-lenity-perspective into death penalty debates, we can resolve them, within the confines of current practice, in favor of *level down*. Justice Stevens took this approach when in a 1987 dissent he accepted the *Gregg* framework but argued that, given the Baldus data, prosecutors should limit capital charges to "the worst of the worst" of *death* penalty defendants—i.e., to defendants who score high on the Baldus culpability scale.[16] The Stevens proposal accommodates current capital sentencing practice, and it does by holding out the prospect of reducing unjustified racial disparities. It would leave capital punishment in place however. We will have an opportunity to consider something more fundamental in Section IV.

Notes

1. Analysis of the distinction between comparative and non-comparative justice adopted here is indebted to Joel Feinberg, "Non-Comparative Justice," *Philosophical Review* 83: 297 (1974).
2. Brian Johnson, Ryan King, Cassia Spohn, "Sociolegal Approaches to the Study of Guilty Pleas and Prosecution," *Annual Review of Law and Social Science* 12: 479 (2016).
3. See *supra* note 16 in Chapter 6.
4. For discussion, see Jeannie Suk Gersen, "The Unintended Consequences of the Stanford *Rape*-Case Recall," *The New Yorker* (June 17, 2016).
5. For discussion, see Jennifer Taub, *Big Dirty Money* 97 (2021).
6. For an analysis of its own procedures (that takes into 4 the *Booker* accommodation, discussed *infra* at note 14 in Chapter 6 and accompanying), see U.S. Sentencing Commission, *Guidelines* (2023).
7. *Booker v. United States*, 543 U.S. 220 (2005).

8. U.S. Sentencing Commission, *Report* 1 (2023).
9. Id.
10. Michael Light, "The Declining Significance of Race in Criminal Sentencing: Evidence from US Federal Courts," *Social Forces* 100: 1110 (2022).
11. Mona Lynch et al., "Prosecutors, Court Communities, and Policy Change: The Impact of Internal DOJ Guidelines on Federal Prosecutorial Practices," *Criminology* 52: 480 (2021).
12. *Gregg v. Georgia*, 428 U.S. 153 (1976).
13. See the statistics discussed in Justice Marshall's *Furman* concurrence, establishing that between 1930 and 1970, 455 Blacks and 48 Whites were executed for rape. 408 U.S. 314, 364 (1972).
14. David Baldus, "Race Discrimination and the Legitimacy of the Death Penalty," *DePaul Law Review* 53: 1411, 1446 n. 136.
15. See *supra* note 16 in Chapter 3 and accompanying text.
16. *McCleskey v. Kemp*, 481 U.S. 279, 357 (Stevens, J., dissenting).

PART IV

Addressing Social Justice Issues Beyond the Administration of Criminal Law (and so Promoting its Fair Operation)

CHAPTER 8

Decriminalization: The Significance of the Principle that Limits State-Imposed Punishment to Acts of Wrongful Force and Fraud

Each of the chapters in the previous section has addressed an issue of comparative justice—racial disparities in policing, racial and gender disparities in sentencing, and class disparities in access to the courts. This chapter considers an issue of *non*-comparative justice. In particular, the chapter examines the claim that the state may *never* criminalize certain types of acts. This kind of inquiry doesn't preclude questions about comparative justice. The former takes priority over the latter, though, for if it's never permissible for the state to punish a given act, then questions about one group's treatment by comparison with another's yield to the more fundamental issues associated with justice under any circumstances.

The questions addressed in the chapter are often discussed by reference to the term *decriminalization*. Over the course of the last two centuries, numerous acts that were once criminalized now no longer are. Blasphemy was once a crime. Possession of alcohol was criminalized (during the Prohibition era of the 1920s). Consensual sodomy among adults was criminalized throughout most American history.[1] Each of these has been decriminalized. In defending this trend, and arguing for its extension, the chapter proposes a general principle: that state penal power is properly deployed only to prohibit acts of wrongful force and fraud (*WFF*). As outlined here, the *WFF* principle allows for the possibility of state

W. C. Heffernan, *Social Justice/Criminal Justice*,
https://doi.org/10.1007/978-3-031-75397-8_8

regulation of certain conduct, as distinguished from criminalization of it. It allows, for instance, for state regulation of the sale and possession of alcoholic beverages, though it rejects the legitimacy of a general criminal prohibition on their possession. Nuanced variations on the *WFF* principle are possible, in other words. At the same time, though, an advocate of this approach stands by a straightforward point: that in a decent society, state power may never be used to coerce behavior by threat of punishment for any purpose other than prevention of the culpable conduct that comes under the heading *wrongful force and fraud*.

This position has a good deal in common with the one John Stuart Mill took when he proposed what he called *the harm principle*. In *On Liberty*, an 1859 essay, Mill argued that the.

> only purpose for which power can rightfully be exercised over any member of a civilised community, against his will, is to prevent harm to others. His own good, either physical or moral, is not a sufficient warrant. He cannot rightfully be compelled to do or forbear because it will be better for him to do so, because it will make him happier, because, in the opinion of others, to do so would be wise, or even right.[2]

The limitation of criminal law to acts of *WFF* is not, however, identical with the limitations Mill endorsed when he argued for the harm principle. This is because Mill's harm principle is best understood as a plea for tolerance—a plea against the use of force (not merely physical force, but also the force of public opinion) when this is deployed to ensure conformity with the dominant social conventions of the day. As defended here, the *WFF* principle is both narrower and more specific than what Mill proposed. It's narrower because the *WFF* principle is concerned with the exercise of state penal power, and not (as Mill also was) with efforts by non-government agents to promote conformity with everyday mores. On the other hand, the principle outlined here is more specific because a limitation of penal authority to acts of *WFF* is more definite than one that speaks generally of harm.

Even with this greater specificity, the *WFF* principle still has fuzzy boundaries. This point has to be conceded, particularly if it is argued (as this chapter does) that the state may use its power to prohibit imminent acts of wrongful force and fraud—i.e., acts that have yet to occur but that would result in serious dislocation were they to occur. Nonetheless, the specificity associated with *WFF* is greater by comparison with the phrase ***harm to others***, for in using that phrase as a criterion to determine the scope of state penal power someone might make a case for criminalizing, say, blasphemy (given the shock it might occasion in members of the public), or alcohol consumption (given its deleterious effect on those in a surrounding area), or consensual sodomy (given the possibility of sexually transmitted disease). The *WFF* principle, while also not offering a conclusive criterion for rejecting criminalization of these acts, at least directs attention to what matters—to what an individual does or may do rather than the effect (or possible effect) of his acts on others.

The chapter that follows contains a three-part defense of the *WFF* principle (and thus a qualified rejection of some features of the harm principle). It begins by examining further the distinction between non-comparative and comparative justice. Although there are many reasons why the distinction matters, it's particularly relevant to social justice issues in the ingestion of controlled substances because of the impact of drug laws on racial minorities. The chapter's first section notes that drug laws have led to disproportionate punishment of Blacks and Hispanics by comparison with Whites when self-report studies about drug use are considered. The section nonetheless argues that this comparative justice perspective should be set aside when thinking about the more general (and non-comparative) question of what should be criminalized, for if a convincing answer to this question is possible, it properly takes precedence over questions of comparative justice.

The second section expands on the distinction between the harm and *WFF* principles. The former is more individualistic in focus than the latter, the section notes. Mill's harm principle points toward a realm of individual choice that stretches beyond the criminal law: it holds out the prospect of protection of autonomous choice in settings where government doesn't wield power—in settings such as the family, religious life, and education, for instance. In contrast, the *WFF* principle is concerned exclusively with the scope of the government's penal power. In defending it, someone takes no stand on contested questions concerning, say, the scope of parental authority or the degree of conformity to sacred doctrine a church may properly demand of its adherents. *WFF*'s focus is exclusively on *the state's* power to impose punishment, in other words.

The third, and longest, section considers the proper scope of this power. If, as argued here, the *WFF* principle can be deployed not merely to prohibit acts that actually cause damage but also that might bring this about, challenging questions arise about how far to go by means of prevention. Three different types of acts will be considered during the course of the chapter: drug-possession, weapons-possession, and speed limits for driving. Criminal penalties concerning each can be classified as *prophylactic* laws in that the limitations they impose might be justified by reference to the possibility of future harm. Each, however, raises different issues as to the scope of legitimate social prophylaxis, so each, I argue, must be approached on its own terms when thinking about the proper scope of state penal power.

From Comparative to Non-Comparative Justice

Assume the following: (i) reliable survey data establishes that Blacks and Hispanics possess a legally prohibited drug at about the same rate as Whites but (ii) Blacks and Hispanics are punished more frequently for the drug's possession than are Whites. If we assume that (i) and (ii) are empirically sound (and there is reason to believe they are[3]), an obvious question of comparative justice arises: what justification can be advanced for the racial disparities at stake here? If no convincing answer to this question is provided, a move from comparative to non-comparative justice might be in order: that is, one might argue that in light of the disparities at stake, the legitimacy of all drug prohibitions might be questioned. An argument along these lines was advanced concerning the death penalty. It's plausible here as well.

A more direct criticism is also pertinent, though: what justification can be advanced for criminalizing any act that doesn't directly threaten others? Possession of a prohibited mind-altering drug can't be characterized as an act of wrongful force; nor can it be characterized as an act of fraud. So why should the state use its penal power at all in this context?

A similar challenge could be posed concerning weapons-possession or high-speed driving. These acts often endanger others. Considered on their own, though, neither involves direct harm to those besides the persons engaging in them. Needless to say, the possibility of an imminent threat to others' safety has to be considered. Because it does, criminalization of these acts needs to be considered—as, of course, does criminalization of drug-possession and alcohol-possession as well. These prophylactic questions take precedence over questions of comparative justice, though, for if no one can properly be subject to state sanction for an act, data about disparate enforcement of a criminal prohibition matters less than questions about the harm that might be done to others.

This is the framework that will inform discussion throughout the remainder of the chapter. A decent society, I assume, limits the use of the criminal sanction to acts that either consist of *WFF* or that have a close connection to this. Needless to say, a great deal hinges on the proximity term employed in this sentence. The principle is clear, though: it limits the punitive power of the state—the power to deprive someone of his liberty through censure of his conduct—to acts that undermine the fair terms of cooperation, acts directly undermine cooperative activity, or are closely related to this.

The Harm Principle Distinguished from the *WFF* Principle

Before turning to discussion of the proximity issues pertinent to the position just taken, it will be helpful to comment further on the distinction between the harm and *WFF* principles. The distinction hinges on the following: on support (offered by an advocate of the harm principle) for a wide scope for the exercise of autonomous decision-making not only in areas overseen by the government but in other areas as well, as distinguished from the position (taken by an advocate of the *WFF* principle) for a more limited principle that deals only with the scope of government power to impose punishment for gravely malicious conduct. This distinction is in turn understandable in terms of two different versions of political pluralism, an individualistic one vs. a position that emphasizes the importance of preserving the state's role in vindicating the obligations of restraint but goes no further than this.

Mill's position favors the former version of pluralism. Mill supports the rights of wives to reach conclusions at odds with those of their husbands, of mature children to disagree with the positions taken by their parents, of church members to challenge the theological doctrine embraced by their pastors, of club members to defect from a club to form another, and so on. In endorsing Tocqueville's fear of the "tyranny of the majority," Mill of course expresses reservations about government efforts to impose a belief system on those within a political community. His concern is broader, though, and because it is, his harm principle can't be read merely as a statement about the proper scope of political/legal power but also as a statement about the attitude of toleration each member of a liberal community should bring to bear on the actions of other communal members. Put differently, Mill worked out the ramifications of individualistic self-determination for a secular world that were implicit in the Protestant reformation which had begun three centuries earlier.[4]

The *WFF* principle is less ambitious in scope, but more compact in its commitment to liberal governance. Unlike the harm principle, it offers no principled objection to the existence of powerful sub-groups within civil society that shape the belief systems of their members, and it thus doesn't point toward the commitment to tolerant individualism that informs Mill's framework. Parents often exercise decisive power over even their adult children, withholding approval or expressing disapproval in order to promote a preferred outcome. Pastors use the prospect of excommunication, or more modestly, the prospect of shunning to shape the behavior of members of their congregations. Teachers also draw on their authority to point students in one direction rather than another. In none of these instances can it be said that wrongful *physical* force is employed. In all of them, however, *emotional* force is at stake, and the result is something more complicated than the atomistic individualism characteristic of Millian individualism. Rather, under the *WFF* principle, the government doesn't use its penal power to determine the beliefs entertained by its citizens (on this point, the two principles converge), but the principle doesn't challenge the power of mediating institutions (the family and religious associations, in particular) to exert emotional force over their members and so to promote shared beliefs and mores.

A proponent of liberal individualism would argue in favor of Mill's position. A proponent liberal group pluralism wouldn't necessarily endorse or support it, however. Because the *WFF* principle has more modest ambitions than does Mill's principle, adoption of *WFF* means only that the advocate doesn't treat it as a framework that favors the full exercise of individual autonomy as a necessary component of a decent society. Put differently, someone taking this position makes a limited point—i.e., that the condemnatory power of the criminal law should be confined to acts that unmistakably interfere with the just interests of other members of the community.

But what about the state's power to regulate behavior rather than punish it? On this issue, Mill's harm principle is genuinely disappointing. In contrast, the *WFF* principle provides a promising way to begin thinking about the scope of the state's coercive authority. Mill's approach is disappointing because state regulation (i.e., the government's exercise of its non-criminal power to set standards for the conduct of communal life) necessarily involves force—not force backed by the threat of penal sanction (this of course is true by definition) but force backed by the threat of fines plus the prospect of active intervention by government agents. The passage from *On Liberty* quoted at the beginning of this chapter doesn't note this distinction. It speaks of *power* without noting that the state can use this to back up a threat of punishment but that it can also use this in non-punitive ways.

One of the virtues of the *WFF* principle is that it presupposes a distinction between the two types of power. This virtue is modest, of course, because an appeal to *WFF* provides no guidance as to what's beyond it—i.e., the proper scope of the government's regulatory authority. A first step toward answering this question is to say that the power to regulate can be justified in light of an important goal: promotion of the public interest. In building on this, we can say that government promotes the public interest by adopting initiatives that optimize the terms of collective life and also by adopting initiatives that protect incapacitated individuals from harming themselves. An appeal to the public interest aims at reconciling the tradeoffs associated with collective life, and it also aims at protecting vulnerable individuals (children, for instance, plus mentally and physically infirm adults) from harming themselves and others. The scope of the terms just used is contestable, of course. But while the terms just are merely suggestive, they're importantly so since they point to the possibility of justifying the exercise of government authority for the betterment of communal life *in the absence of the criminal sanction—i.e., in the absence of the power to condemn (and thus to stigmatize).*

Questions of Degree

Regulation serves as an attractive alternative to criminal law in each of the settings mentioned earlier: driving a car, drug-possession, and weapons-possession. Of the three topics, safe-driving rules serve as a particularly helpful way to begin thinking about the line-drawing issues that arise when moving from regulatory power to use of the criminal sanction. Given their size, cars pose an obvious danger to pedestrians and also to people driving other cars. It's clearly in the public interest to regulate virtually every facet of their use. In some settings, the criminal law also must come into play, for the phrase *wrongful force* is clearly pertinent when intentional vehicular harm is at stake.

Difficult line-drawing issues arise when we turn to negligence. The concept of negligence lies at the borderline of wrongfulness. Once negligence is under consideration, it becomes necessary to focus on the legitimacy of social prophylaxis—in particular, to think about the use of criminal sanctions to promote public safety even when an individual's conduct isn't profoundly culpable. Regulatory measures are of course appropriate here, but under what circumstances is criminal law *also* appropriate given the condemnation associated with it? The answer hinges on the degree of risk someone takes as well as the endangerment possibilities associated with a given object. As far as cars are concerned, if someone drives at a speed that poses a serious and immediate risk to the safety of other motorists or pedestrians, that driver's conduct can be classified as sufficiently culpable to justify use of the criminal law for preventive purposes on behalf of the public. A standard such as this is context-specific, of course. An immediate risk to pedestrians in a city business district is posed by a much slower speed than is a risk to drivers in the midst of flat desert terrain, so the speed at which driving merits criminalization for prophylactic purposes will vary.

To note this, however, is not to identify the speed limit that should be established in either context. All that can be said confidently is that regulatory rules (involving license-loss and fines) should govern speeds below the line drawn and that criminal law should govern speeds substantially beyond it. The word *substantially* perhaps shouldn't be determined in advance but should be identified only by referring to a standard of criminal negligence (*a gross deviation from the standard of care employed by a reasonable person*) that generates variable conclusions depending on the setting in which it's applied. Even this may be insufficient, for it might be argued that the fictitious entity called *the reasonable person* drives slightly above the speed limit and that a gross deviation—concededly, a less than precise phrase—must occur to warrant criminalization. Whatever framework is employed, it's essential to acknowledge that questions of degree are inherently contestable in line-drawing settings of the kind we're considering. But while some arbitrariness is inescapable, it can nonetheless be affirmed that at a certain point, criminal law's condemnatory measures may properly be used to protect the public from negligent driving that poses a substantial risk to the safety of others since this can be confidently classified as *wrongful conduct*.

This discussion of speeding sets the stage for thinking about the questions that arise when thinking about regulation of controlled substances (i.e., objects that, on ingestion, can alter the mental or physical state of those consuming them). Virtually any ingestible object can have this effect (chewing gum can lead to tooth decay, for example)—thus the need for a comprehensive regulatory framework in this context. As with speeding, it's clear that criminalization is in order for intentional or reckless acts that produce substantial harm to others when ingested. Also, as with speeding the question arises as to when criminalization is in order for negligence.

Here, though, two different facets of negligence are at issue, one having to do with production of an ingestible object, the other with its consumption. As for the former, the standard outlined earlier is also appropriate in this context: negligent production of a substance that can be consumed should be subject to criminalization whenever there is a substantial risk of serious harm to someone who might consume it. As for the latter, a fundamentally different set of considerations is pertinent, for as long as the harm involved is limited to the person consuming the object, the *WFF* principle provides no justification for criminalization. Regulation is in order of course, but as long as the producers of a good warn consumers about the risks involved, there is no reason to hold consumers criminally responsible for the harm they do themselves.

The decriminalization of marijuana that's occurred during the past two decades illustrates how this would work. Assuming that producers and vendors of marijuana sell the product with satisfactory warnings about the risks involved, there is no reason given the *WFF* principle to punish the person consuming it. Substantial harm to a consumer's organs and thought processes may result from prolonged, intensive consumption of marijuana.[5] This isn't an appropriate trigger for invocation of the state's power to punish, however. If someone does sufficient harm to him/herself, the state may use its regulatory power for rehabilitative purposes, but punishment is unacceptable if the *WFF* principle is taken seriously.

This framework can readily be extended to controlled substances—heroin and cocaine, for instance—whose possession is currently criminalized. Because possession of these drugs is now subject to the criminal sanction, consumers who purchase them have no opportunity to know about their composition or to review legally enforceable warnings about the risks they pose. In adopting a regulatory framework and forswearing criminalization, the state would reduce substantially the risk of self-harm that accompanies consumption of these drugs. Serious risks would remain, of course. Assuming, though, that these risks are limited to the drugs' consumers, there is no reason for the state to use its criminal power to interfere in this context. Thousands of people drink themselves dead every year; thousands more bring on lung cancer through intensive smoking. These are properly subjects for persuasion (for extended advertising campaigns, for instance)—and, when necessary, for rehabilitation undertaken subject to regulatory oversight. The substances now subject to the criminal sanction shouldn't be treated differently.

But what if some substance—perhaps one that's currently consumed or perhaps one that's yet to be created—is so potent that its consumption would create an immediate risk of violence against others? If this could be demonstrated, then the *WFF* principle would be pertinent, for someone consuming such a drug would come sufficiently close to resembling a human time bomb as to make it justifiable for the state not merely to use its regulatory power to protect the public but also its penal power prophylactically to take steps to prevent future cases of the same kind. At present, though, there's no reported drug of this kind—i.e., there's nothing comparable to a car being driven through a crowded business district at 100 miles per hour. Because there isn't, we can grant that there's a notional possibility of a "human time-bomb" drug, but that there's nothing more.

Rather, in turning from the notional to the realistic, we can say that the *WFF* principle provides a plausible framework for decriminalizing what are currently called controlled substances, that regulating the production and consumption of these substances in much the same way that alcohol and cigarettes are regulated would have the beneficial side effect of eliminating incarceration of people who are being punished merely for their possession (thus contributing to reduction of racial and class disparities in state-imposed punishment), and that attaching criminal penalties (as is now the case with alcohol) to people who commit acts of violence after consuming such substances would draw appropriately on the *WFF* principle, thereby bringing it into line with the law's treatment of other ingestible substances (alcohol, for instance). In adopting this approach, we would have no need to consider the preference for liberal individualism that informs Mill's harm principle. We would need only think about the proper function of the criminal law, which is for government to protect the public from acts of *WFF.*

In conclusion, we should think about the pertinence of the *WFF* principle to the criminalization of firearms possession. Many of the factors worth considering here are similar to those discussed earlier. Like cars, firearms are inherently dangerous objects; they thus are properly subject to comprehensive regulation. Also, if a firearm is used in an act of force, this is a sufficient reason for enhancing the penalties associated with the act. And finally, there are important prophylactic considerations for criminalizing the possession of firearms given the harm that can result from careless ownership of them. One factor is distinctive, however: their utility for purposes of self-defense. This consideration has to be taken into account when thinking about regulating and criminalizing their possession, and because it must be considered a different set of calculations is in order than those considered in the two earlier cases.

The self-defense issue is relevant to regulation *and* criminalization. Because a firearm is sometimes essential to self-defense, regulations must not be so onerous as to prevent its acquisition. Similarly, criminal prohibitions mustn't stand in the way of exercising the right of self-defense. These general points need to be supplemented by contextual ones. That is, when the rate of firearm possession increases (indeed, particularly when the rate of *illegal* firearm possession increases), the rationale for lawful ownership of a firearm for purposes of self-defense becomes stronger as well. To note this is to focus on a tragic feature of the right of self-defense. A government that's failed to limit the illegal possession of firearms has failed, at least to a significant degree, to perform one of its essential duties—i.e., its obligation to protect citizens from the risk of predatory acts of violence. When this occurs, regulations and criminal prohibitions must be adjusted to take this into account.

None of this means, though, that regulations and prophylactic criminal prohibitions are impermissible for firearms when these have no reasonable relationship to self-defense. The qualifications just noted are pertinent primarily to handguns—pertinent, in other words, to settings in which an individual may need to defend him/herself against acts of armed aggression by other individuals. Firearms that can kill large groups of people may be banned entirely, then, and thus may be subject to strict criminal prohibition. Put differently, because automatic and semi-automatic weapons are offensive, not defensive, devices, they have no legitimate standing as far as the *WWF* principle is concerned.

It's possible to expand application of the *WFF* principle and so think about it in other settings as well. Enough has been said here, however, to establish that the *WFF* principle is relevant to regulation *and* criminalization decisions concerning the difficult questions of degree that arise in numerous cases involving harm to one's self and harm to others—and so to establish, in particular, that there's no need to think in terms of comparative justice when considering matters such as drug and weapons possession laws but instead to assess them in terms of the broad-based *WWF* principle that properly governs the criminalization decisions that must be made in a decent society.

Notes

1. Surprisingly, there is no contemporary history of this long-term trend. For a decades-old book that anticipates recent developments, see David Richards, *Sex, Drugs, Death and the Law* (1986).
2. John Stuart Mill, *On Liberty* Chap. 1 (1859).
3. For discussion, see Patrick Langan, *Racial Disparity in U.S. Drug Arrests* (Bureau of Justice Statistics, 1995), @ bjs.ojp/gov/library/publications/tacial-disparity-us-drug-arrests.
4. For discussion of Tocqueville's influence on Mill, see Alan Ryan, *On Tocqueville: Democracy and America* (2014).
5. For a review of marijuana's side effects, see National Institute on Drug Abuse, *Cannabis: Drug Facts* (2019), @ nida.nih.go/publications/drugfacts/cannabis-marijuana.

CHAPTER 9

Rethinking the Prosecution, and Sentencing, of White-Collar Offenders

Writing in 1940 in the *American Sociological Review*, Edwin Sutherland proposed a class-based framework for thinking about the administration of criminal law. "The crimes of the lower class are handled by policemen, prosecutors, and judges, with penal sanctions in the form of fines, imprisonment, and death," Sutherland wrote.

> The crimes of the upper class result in no official action at all, or result in suits for damages in civil courts, or are handled by inspectors, or by administrative boards or commissions, with penal sanctions in the form of warnings, orders to cease and desist, occasional rescinding of a license, and in extreme cases with fines and prison sentences.[1]

Sutherland's distinction—violent crime addressed by regular police vs. white-collar crime addressed by specialized police, if addressed at all—was quickly incorporated into criminological theory, along with a class-based corollary: that violent crime is typically (though not invariably) committed by those of limited resources and that white-collar crime is the province of the wealthy as well as the middle class. Or, to qualify this in an important way, the Sutherland distinction informs academic discourse about criminal law, though it perhaps still doesn't influence discussion beyond universities, for conversations about criminal law conducted in newspapers and on television usually refer to *crime* simpliciter and so leave the impression that only acts of violence matter when talking about the subject at all.

W. C. Heffernan, *Social Justice/Criminal Justice*,
https://doi.org/10.1007/978-3-031-75397-8_9

In remarks published a generation after Sutherland introduced his distinction, James Q. Wilson reinforced this impression about crime. I give "principal attention," Wilson stated in *Thinking about Crime*, published in 1975, "to predatory street crime rather than to 'white-collar' crime." Wilson justified this point by arguing that.

> predatory crime, in particular crime committed by strangers on innocent victims, causes the kind of fear that drives people apart from one another and thus impedes or even prevents the formation of meaningful communities." Because "all nations punish, in the name of the state, theft and unjustified violence," Wilson wrote, "one should not apologize for writing a book about predatory crime and leaving to others the important task of writing about 'white-collar' crime.[2]

This chapter takes a different approach. In doing so, it defends the premise that informs the entire book—i.e., that the acts properly addressed by a central enforcement agency include not only those involving wrongful force but also fraud. Wilson relies on an unnecessary dichotomy, the chapter thus suggests, for there is no need to focus *either* on wrongful force *or* on fraud. Or at least Wilson appears to rely on this unnecessary distinction, for as can readily be noted on reading his remarks carefully, Wilson doesn't mention the term *fraud*. It's possible that Wilson would have conceded that the punishment imposed by "all nations" (his criterion for determining what matters when thinking about crime) not only addresses acts of wrongful force (he mentions theft and unjustified violence) but also acts of systematic deception—i.e., fraud—and possible he would even have conceded that theft can be carried out by means of fraud *as well as* force. It's possible, of course, that Wilson would have granted these points. But because he didn't note them—and because he drew a stark contrast between violent crime and white-collar crime (a term he discussed only by derisive use of quotation marks)—one can't say for sure. All that's certain is that Wilson emphatically rejected the class-based distinction at the heart of Sutherland's comments. Violent crime (mostly the province of the resource-limited) matters. Crimes of deception (mostly the province of the well-to-do) don't.

Because a decent society must take both kinds of crime seriously and because earlier chapters have focused primarily on violent crime, this chapter critically examines the subject Wilson relegated to quotation marks. Its first section discusses definitional points, in particular the scope of the term *fraud*. The next section deals with statistical issues: it asks about the frequency of white-collar crime. The third section considers enforcement problems, in particular the resource shortages that are often encountered when investigating financial crimes. The fourth and final section then turns to difficult questions of comparative justice: it contrasts the maximum sentences imposed for white-collar, as distinguished from, violent crime. The discussion throughout the chapter aims at integrating analysis of both types of crime. It affirms the significance of the *WFF* formula, thereby supporting the core premise that a decent society is one that addresses all types of wrongful acts that undermine the fair terms of cooperation.

Definitional Issues

The term *white-collar crime* has fuzzy boundaries, thus making it essential to consider its scope before turning to enforcement questions. The term is often used to refer not merely to acts that come under the heading of fraud but also to refer to acts such as environmental degradation, price-fixing, embezzlement, and tax evasion. None of these can be classified as fraud within the narrow meaning of the term, for when it's used in its strict sense *fraud* refers to an "intentionally deceptive action designed to provide the perpetrator with an unlawful gain or to deny a right to a victim."[3] This standard definition of the term points to something broader, though, for once it's granted that fraud is concerned with "intentionally deceptive action" (a component of the definition just provided), one can add that even though activities such as price-fixing and insider-trading don't come within the narrow sense of the word, they nonetheless rely on deception of some kind in order to achieve their purpose. After all, price-fixing and insider-trading aren't carried out in the open. Deception is one of their key features, though the deception essential to each is carried out in a different way and for different purposes than in cases of fraud as that term is used in the narrow sense of the term. It's because this is true that the final *F* in *WFF* can be understood to stand for fraud in a strict sense *and also* in a broader one. We thus can say that fraud isn't simply a specific category of crime but that it's also a suggestive term that captures a theme that informs the (also suggestive) label *white-collar crime*, for everything associated with this label relies on deception of one kind or another.

A list employed by the FBI for investigating corporate fraud confirms this point. The FBI list includes some of the different kinds of crime that come within the narrow sense of the term *fraud*: fraudulent trades designed to inflate profits and hide losses, for instance, financial institution mortgage fraud, and health care fraud. But the FBI list of corporate fraud crimes also includes other acts that do *not* contain the word *fraud* even though they have a clear affinity with the ones just mentioned: insider-trading and kickbacks, misuse of corporate property for personal gain, and falsification of net asset values.[4] Someone might argue that because the first set of crimes mentioned in this paragraph comes with the label *fraud* and the second set does not, only the first should be analyzed as examples of fraud for definitional purposes.

To take this approach, however, is to disregard not only the obvious similarities, grounded in the more general theme of deception for purposes of financial gain, between the two clusters of crime, but to disregard the FBI's placement of all the crimes just mentioned under the heading *corporate fraud*. Moreover, in taking this approach, someone would disregard something else of significance revealed by the FBI list. This is because the list alerts us to the possibility that fraud, broadly conceived, is committed by organizations (corporations and partnerships, for instance) as well as individuals, thus making it a subject with ramifications for personal and institutional liability.

Given these points, the sensible approach is to grant the claim made earlier—i.e., that there are narrow and broad senses of *fraud*—and so to grant that the capacious, though admittedly vague, phrase *white-collar crime* has now become part of everyday discourse, and that it includes the narrow sense of deceit for personal gain in a financial transaction as its core concern plus broader senses of deceitful acts for personal or organizational financial advantage as penumbral concerns. The remainder of the chapter relies on this definitional premise.

Monitoring the Incidence of White-Collar Crime

How widespread is fraud given this broad conception of the term? There is no reliable national database that reports on the different types of white-collar crime. The Uniform Crime Reports (UCR), published by the FBI, provide relatively reliable information about trends in violent crime—highly reliable data about homicide and somewhat less reliable information about other crimes such as rape and robbery. Even when it deals in a less than wholly convincing way with some specific violent crimes, though, the UCR is still noteworthy because it offers a plausible overall portrait of trends in violent crime.

The same cannot be said of the UCR's data on white-collar crime. Although the UCR contains data concerning some kinds of white-collar crime trends (it deals with credit-card fraud, impersonation, and wire fraud, for instance), the information presented is viewed with considerable skepticism by many criminologists. There are many reasons why this skepticism is warranted. Victims of white-collar crimes sometimes don't grasp what's been done to them. When they do, they often don't contact government authorities. And even when victims actually want to report what's happened to them, they may not know how to proceed, for the police are primarily concerned with violent crime (and also with other acts that aren't defined as criminal but that matter a great deal in communal life) while the officials who address white-collar crimes are considerably less accessible than the police.

This doesn't mean, though, that there's nothing but a black-hole problem here. On the contrary, inferences can be drawn from the fragmentary data currently available, inferences that make it possible to generalize on specific types of crimes and even to generalize more broadly on the incidence of all crimes that come under the broad heading *white-collar crime*. Both types of inferences merit consideration. We should begin with a broad generalization about the frequency of the phenomenon. "Although most scholarship in the field tends to be more conceptual and qualitative in nature," Sally Simpson remarks,

> the few quantitative studies that have been conducted have produced some uniform findings: (1) the amount of white-collar and corporate crime is extensive, (2) a large portion of offenders are recidivists, (3) similar to street offenders, a small number of offenders account for the bulk of offending, and (4) in some regulatory arenas (such as the environment), most regulated companies generally are law-abiding.[5]

In building on these cautious generalizations, we should note two specific points—limited generalizations, as they can be called. The first has to do with the question of trends. While UCR data concerning the white-collar crimes noted above suggests that their rate of occurrence may be declining, self-report surveys (the IC3 Annual Report, for instance) point in the opposite direction.[6] One might hypothesize that this latter trend is attributable to greater public awareness of the possibility of victimization (and thus that the crimes reported in the UCR actually are declining). Alternatively, though, one might hypothesize that the self-report surveys point accurately toward an increase in white-collar crime, for it's possible that technological change has facilitated predatory financial crimes and that victims of these crimes are increasingly aware of the harm they're suffering. Because there's a certain degree of plausibility to each of these hypotheses, the soundest verdict to reach is that, in the absence of better methods of investigation, it *may be* the case that alterations in technology have made white-collar crime more common with the passage of time, though this is far from certain.

The other limited generalization worth noting has to do with the identity of victims of white-collar crime, in particular the identity of the victims of tax fraud and other frauds on the government. Although reporting on crimes such as credit-card and wire fraud is somewhat scanty, reporting on frauds against the government is scantier still. For this, we have to rely almost entirely on estimates generated by an examination of government audits of tax returns. Those estimates suggest (the verb is apt) that a vast amount of revenue is unreported in tax returns and that a significant amount of money is secured through fraudulent misrepresentations for government services, particularly Medicare and Medicaid. Furthermore, the data suggest (again, nothing stronger should be said) that, in dollar amounts, rich taxpayers play a disproportionately large role as far as government losses are concerned. Recent research has established that under the Trump administration, the IRS audited more Earned Income Tax Credit recipients (i.e., low-income wage earners) than millionaires—yet the government loses more in revenue from the latter than from the former.[7] The amounts at stake can't be conclusively determined. They rely on reasonable estimates, however, thus casting modest light on a black hole in contemporary criminology.

Resource Shortages in White-Collar Crime Law Enforcement

Why is it that so little is known about the incidence of fraud against the government? One answer is obvious: because harm is suffered by the public at large, there's no single victim at stake in this kind of fraud. But two other (complementary) answers also need to be considered. One is that fraud of any kind, not merely fraud against the government, is particularly hard to identify—i.e., private citizens are rarely in a position to know the universe of facts relevant to a given transaction with a third party and thus rarely knowledgeable enough to report a fraud. And the other answer is that, when government is the victim, it needs substantial resources to demonstrate that it's been cheated—and these resources are frequently unavailable.

This final point takes us to the *ostrich problem* in white-collar law enforcement: to the factors that have left the government ignorant of criminal activities because of legislative decisions (i.e., decisions by government officials) that have denied it the wherewithal to conduct thorough investigation of the money to which it's entitled. The ostrich problem extends even to frauds in which private parties have been victimized, for there are important white-collar criminal cases (the Bernard Madoff Ponzi scheme is an example[8]) in which government agencies have been alerted to questionable activities but have not undertaken an investigation, in part because of resource shortages. Important as these cases are, it will be helpful to concentrate on resource-shortage issues that arise when the government itself has been shortchanged, for it's here that we encounter a particularly serious conflict of interest in white-collar crime: the political leverage privileged members of society exercise in persuading legislators not to appropriate the funds needed to investigate criminal activity by the rich. This leverage may extend even to violent crime: it may include efforts by privileged members of society to foreclose investigation of acts such as murder and rape. It's particularly important as far as taxes are concerned, though, for here we encounter a chokehold on the apparatus of state penal power that, while not as dramatic as the state capture pattern that existed under Jim Crow, nonetheless bears a strong resemblance to it given the way in which it insulates prosperous members of society from investigation into their illegal acts.

A current events example helps illustrate this point. During the 2010s, a decade in which Republicans controlled one or both houses of Congress for all but two years, staffing for the IRS was reduced by 22%. During this time, audits went down by almost 50%; by the end of the decade, only 0.59% of tax returns were audited.[9] The deterrence ramifications of this decline are self-evident, for as the likelihood of detection decreases (in any setting, not merely in taxation), the likelihood of compliance with the law decreases as well.

In the early 2020s, with Democrats controlling the presidency and both houses of Congress, an effort was made to add to the IRS staff—and so to conduct more audits. Experts estimated that each dollar invested along these lines would more than pay for itself in terms of increased revenue. An estimate (by the Congressional Budget Office) placed the ratio at 1.5 dollars for each dollar invested. Relying more on this, the Biden administration successfully persuaded Congress to include enhanced funding for the IRS in the Inflation Reduction Act of 2021. When Republicans regained control of the House in the 2022 election, their first legislative act in January 2023 was to vote to repeal this extra funding. This was only a symbolic gesture, of course, since President Biden announced that he would veto this if the legislation ever reached him. But the Republican efforts didn't end here. When the Biden administration asked Congress in November 2023 to appropriate 14 billion dollars to help Israel respond to attacks by Hamas, the Republican House did so only by stripping an equal amount from IRS. Here, too, there was no prospect of success (and the Congressional Budget Office concluded that a 14 billion reduction in funding for IRS would lead to a reduction in 25 billion dollars in revenue over a ten-year period).[10] There's an important sense, though, that the legislative futility of these Republican efforts is beside the point. Rather, what matters is that these efforts underscore the determination of the most advantaged members of society to use their political power to preserve and extend the advantages they already enjoy. In this instance, the efforts failed, but this matters less in the long run than the general point at stake here: that legislative power is routinely deployed by the most prosperous members of society to provide insulation from the possibility of criminal liability.

This point is pertinent to settings other than tax fraud. It has a bearing on investigations into Medicare and Medicaid fraud, for instance, and also on investigations into fraudulent as well as defective performance of government defense contracts. A critic would grant, of course, that there are only limited resources available for investigating shortcomings pertinent to virtually any type of crime. However, as long as there is good reason to believe that money due the government can be retrieved in any setting, there is also good reason to increase the resources to investigate the circumstances for doing so. Indeed, whenever extra resources are *not* invested in this context, we can say that an obvious imbalance persists in the social justice/criminal justice equation.

Sentencing White-Collar Offenders

One of the longest criminal sentences handed down in American legal history was the one for 150 years imposed on Bernard Madoff in 2009. Madoff's sentence was not, however, representative of trends in white-collar cases. By and large, the longest sentences of convicted white-collar offenders are shorter than the longest sentences for violent crime. Moreover, criminal prosecutions in white-collar cases are sometimes forgone in favor of civil penalties, an option almost never employed in violent crime cases. Because an apples-and-oranges problem arises when assessing the harm associated with white-collar as distinguished from violent crime, it's essential to begin reflection on sentencing in this context by asking whether it's even possible to compare prosecutorial practices for the two types of crimes. This section relies on a claim that comparative justice considerations are at least partially relevant to sentencing issues in both contexts. After reviewing the argument for this qualified version of comparative justice, we will turn to details of white-collar prosecution and sentencing.

Even if one were to say that James Q. Wilson shouldn't have relegated white-collar crime to a marginal role in criminal justice, one might nonetheless contend that the two categories of crime—white-collar and violent—are so different in nature and effect that there's no point in comparing sentencing patterns relevant to them. To say this is to advance a point about incommensurability. This claim has some merit (the differences are of course significant); at the same time, though, it disregards a generic similarity, for it's possible to make comparisons within a general category while nonetheless allowing for more fine-grained differences between items in that category. Someone who eats both apples and oranges can say, for instance, *I should rethink my intake of fruit* and thus increase or decrease his/her consumption of one by comparison with the other—and do so while never moving beyond the category *fruit.* When thinking along these lines, this person might say *I should level up by eating more apples by comparison with oranges* or say *I should level down by eating fewer oranges by comparison with apples.* In each instance, one kind of fruit serves as a baseline for rethinking consumption of the other (ascorbic vs. citric acid), and though this baseline would still involve incommensurables, it could still be analyzed in terms of commensurable physiological effects.

It's in this sense that comparison is possible within a category of otherwise incommensurable items. In applying this framework to sentencing (i.e., by comparing sentences for white-collar and violent crime), we should begin with a straightforward point: that white-collar crime has long been subject to less severe sanctions than violent crime. Table 4, contained in the Appendix, reviews the consistent difference between the two categories in terms of sentence length and the number of cases convicted in federal courts. The ratios of sentence length have decreased from four to one to less than three to one in recent years. In effect, sentences have relied on the premise that the harm done by violent crime is three times more serious than the harm done by white-collar crime.

Well, perhaps. If we take preferences into account, it has to be granted that people would prefer to be defrauded of their life savings than to be killed—and thus that murder should be placed at the top of any sentencing scale. After this, though, sentencing questions become more complex. Indeed, it may be that sentencers would concede uncertainty here. Few people convicted of murder, for instance, have received 150-year sentences—the sentence Madoff received for his white-collar crimes.

Second, it might be argued that, if culpability considerations are set aside, greater leniency for white-collar crimes is in order since these can be deterred by the threat of financial sanctions as well as imprisonment whereas violent crimes (most of which are committed by people who are judgment-proof) can only be deterred by the prospect of imprisonment. There is of course some plausibility to this point as well. It's counterbalanced by another, however, for if it's agreed that white-collar criminality is harder to detect than violent crime, it might reasonably be said that sentences should be longer for this kind of activity in order to deter it.

Another hypothesis merits consideration, then—the possibility that racial and class biases improperly influence sentencers when approaching both kinds of crime. We noted earlier that racial bias appears to influence sentencing in all criminal cases—i.e., we saw (in Chapter 7) that, over the past two decades, similarly situated Black defendants receive sentences nearly 13% longer than White defendants.[11] To this, we can add a further hypothesis: that upper class defendants (who typically have stronger community ties as well as superior legal representation) probably benefit from a similar bias. In taking both points into account, we can readily reject the trend already underway—to *level up* by making white-collar sentences more similar to those for violent crime. But should we adopt *level down*? If by this phrase, someone is suggesting modest, incremental change that takes current practice as the baseline for reasoning, the answer is *no*—or at least, this is the answer if our aim is to create a decent society (and this of course is the informing concern of the chapters in section IV), for current practice is already harshly punitive, even if it's less so for white-collar than for violent crime.

What we should instead conclude is that, first, more government resources should be allocated to investigating white-collar crime; second, the increased revenue gained from prosecuting various frauds against the government (tax, Medicare, Medicaid, and defense procurement, for instance) should be deployed to fund social justice initiatives; and third, *level down*, understood as a term that advocates incremental change, sets too modest a goal for criminal sentencing in a decent society, though it nonetheless points in the right direction. By addressing directly the phenomenon of mass incarceration, the next chapter outlines a program of structural change, one that links decarceration to long-lasting social justice initiatives.

Notes

1. Edwin Sutherland, "White Collar Criminality," *American Sociological Review* 5: 1 (1940).
2. James Q. Wilson, *Thinking about Crime* xxiii-xxiv (rev. ed. 2013).
3. See *Investopedia* @ Investopedia.com/terms/fraud/terms.
4. See FBI, *What We Investigate: White-Collar Crime* @ fbi-gov/investigate.
5. Sally Simpson, "Making Sense of White-collar Crime: Theory and Research," *Ohio State Journal of Criminal Law* 8: 481, 482 (2011).
6. For discussion of flaws in determining the incidence of crimes of deception, see Ishan Mehta, "The Need for Better Metrics on Cybercrime," *Third Way* (October 2019) @ thirdway.org/memo/the-need-for-better-metrics-on-cybercrime.
7. See Americans for Tax Fairness, "New Analysis Shows Trump-Era IRS Audited Low-Income Workers at a Higher Rate than Millionaires" @americansfortaxfairness.org/new-anaysis-shows-Trump-era-IRS-audited-low-income-workers-at-a-higher-rate-than-millio naires.

8. For an account of the government's failure (despite multiple warnings) to investigate Madoff, see Diana Henriques, *The Wizard of Lies* (2011).
9. See Paul Kiel and Jesse Eisenger, "How the IRS Was Gutted," *Pro Publica* December 11, 2018 @ propublica.org/article/how-the-irs-was-gutted.
10. For discussion of this issue, see Robert Goulder, "Modernizing the IRS through the Inflation Reduction Act," *Forbes*, February 24, 2024 @ forbes.com/sites/taxnotes/2024.
11. See *supra* note 8 in Chapter 3 and accompanying text.

CHAPTER 10

Addressing the Problem of Mass Incarceration: Penal Parsimony and the Possibility of Broad-Based Social Justice Initiatives

Reducing racial and class disparities in the administration of criminal law will contribute to the creation of a minimally decent society. So too will repeal of drug possession laws. And so too will stricter enforcement of anti-fraud laws. By themselves, though, none of these steps will produce a society that can be classified as genuinely decent—or at least none will do so while mass incarceration remains a defining feature of the legal system. That is, even if racial and class disparities are meaningfully addressed, even if drug laws are radically overhauled, and even if substantial steps are taken to address white-collar crime, only minimal social decency will be achieved if measures aren't also adopted that reduce dependence on imprisonment as a method of social control. At present, the United States has nearly two million people—slightly less than two-thirds of 1% of its entire population—confined in prisons and jails.[1] The remedies proposed in earlier chapters address the racial and class composition of the incarcerated, and they address other important issues as well. They don't address the sheer volume of imprisonment, though. The remedies about to be discussed can't be adopted through internal reform of the criminal law. They require legislation: they require, in other words, a broad-based commitment to social justice, a commitment possible only in a decent society.

W. C. Heffernan, *Social Justice/Criminal Justice*,
https://doi.org/10.1007/978-3-031-75397-8_10

This chapter examines two different ways of limiting the scope of mass incarceration. The first has to do with the prison population itself—i.e., the chapter considers various measures that come under the heading of *penal parsimony* (steps that restrain, without wholly eliminating, the state's exercise of its power to punish). The second set of remedies considered here has to do with initiatives that make criminal activity less likely—i.e., the chapter considers *social justice initiatives* (i.e., steps that enhance fair equality of opportunity).

These are complementary measures. Penal parsimony, a term that can incorporate the points made earlier about accountability, refers not only to programs that reduce the intake of inmates but also to policies that authorize the early discharge of those already imprisoned. It thus addresses congestion issues in the current legal system. Social justice initiatives, a term that, among other things, refers to policies that promote fair equality of opportunity (FEO) for young people and also to those that promote full employment for adults, reduce the likelihood of criminal offending. The first set of measures is important in the short- and medium term. The second is best understood as a long-term investment in human capital, an investment that, in time, will gradually make the first one less urgent. Each accepts, albeit reluctantly, the legitimacy of state-imposed punishment. Each, however, relies on the premise that the state can't depend primarily on coercion to ensure conformity with the law. Essential to the initiatives discussed here, in other words, is the premise that a genuinely decent society must rely on the wise deployment of resources to promote voluntary compliance with the obligations of restraint. The possibility of such a society depends only incidentally on the prospect of coercive force. What matters critically is the adoption of measures that ensure inclusion of everyone involved.

The chapter that follows contains three sections. The first chapter discusses the vague, but also suggestive, term *mass incarceration*. Though far from self-defining, the term highlights a key feature of American public policy and, to a lesser extent, the policy of other advanced industrial societies—i.e., that from the late twentieth century onward, governments in these societies have increasingly relied on imprisonment as a device of social control. In challenging what is still something of a reflexive reaction to criminality, the first section suggests that the threshold premise of penal parsimony—i.e., that imprisonment should be treated as a tragic event, one that merits consideration only if other options are unavailing and that, if adopted at all, should be authorized only for the shortest reasonable time—must be treated as the starting step for thinking about incarceration.

This proposition is advanced only in programmatic form in the chapter's first section. The second and third sections flesh it out, with the second discussing the steps that must be followed if penal parsimony is to be translated into workable public policy and the third discussing social justice initiatives that promote fair equality of opportunity. The focus throughout is on measures that promote more than minimal decency in social life. An ideal society would be crime-free and so would have no need to consider the programmatic possibilities outlined here. This chapter, in contrast, considers something more realistic—the near certainty that violations of the obligations of restraint will continue to undermine the fair terms of cooperation but the prospect of nonetheless creating an institutional structure that responds in minimally coercive fashion to *WFF*.

The Vague, but Nonetheless Suggestive, Term *Mass Incarceration*

Commentary on punishment typically relies on an illusion of precision, one in which a criminal sanction is said to be *proportioned* to a legal offense. If this proportionality consideration could be used to determine exactly the sanction for an offense, it would definitively resolve questions about whether someone is being *over-* or *underpunished*, for the offense itself would dictate the sanction to be imposed. But it can't. Proportionality, a mathematical term, refers to an exactly determinable relationship between numbers (as in *six is to four as three is to two*), but nothing of this kind is possible for punishment, or at least nothing of this kind is possible when a sanction is rationed out in terms of time of incarceration, for there's nothing proportionate about two or three (or any other number of) years of imprisonment for an act such as armed robbery or aggravated assault. Sanctions such as these may seem *appropriate* or *condign*. To use these terms, though, is to rely on an intuition about the proper fit between an offense and a sanction. It isn't to rely on a mathematical relationship between one number and another.

This is not to say that an appeal to proportionality should be set aside entirely when thinking about punishment. Rather, it's to suggest that there's an inescapable (and frequently unacknowledged) element of vagueness in all discussions of the subject. That vagueness is manifestly present when we turn to the concept of mass incarceration, for this term piles vagueness on vagueness: vagueness in individual cases (given the uncertainties that arise in determining the sanction to be imposed for virtually any act of wrongdoing) and vagueness in surveying the entire legal system (given the uncertainties that arise when sentences are aggregated, with the term *mass* triggered once an arbitrary threshold of individual cases is crossed).

Although the terms involved are imprecise, the statistics are clear. During the last half-century, the American prison population increased by 700%. Table 5 charts its rapid rise throughout the late twentieth century and its modest decline in this century. The preceding chapters have also discussed principles of penal parsimony, though only in a scattered way. This chapter brings them together for purposes of systematic discussion. Adoption of these principles, or at least, adoption of the principles in stringent form won't merely reverse the trend toward mass incarceration; they will transform it. By integrating social justice considerations into the administration of criminal law, they will make it possible to examine criminal justice as a genuinely autonomous subject, one that can be studied without reference to the racial and class biases discussed in the chapters of section III.

Penal Parsimony

Writing in 1974, Norval Morris argued that principles of penal parsimony should guide policymakers in making incarceration and discharge decisions.[2] With fifty years' hindsight, we can see how sound Morris's core concern was—and how it should have been adopted when initially proposed. The four principles outlined below are all compatible with the animating idea of penal parsimony, though they draw on penological initiatives proposals introduced after Morris wrote in the 1970s. They are outlined first in stringent form, then in milder form.

A stringent version of penal parsimony Two key principles have already been introduced. These are: (i) State officials should consider the possibility of punishment only if they determine that someone is accountable for harm (in the form of *WFF*) done to someone else. (ii) They should do so by reference to a culpability scale, one that treats murder as presumptively the most serious crime, rape as second in severity, aggravated assault as third, etc., with the presumptions just mentioned subject to rebuttal given the individualizing circumstances of a case.

In adding to these principles, we can say that (iii) punishment by imprisonment amounts to a deeply troubling curtailment of individual liberty. Because it is, we should add that (iv) the exercise in extended domination essential to imprisonment must be disfavored absent (a) clear evidence of serious wrongdoing and/or (b) the absence of reasonable alternatives for protecting the public from further instances of this. On this analysis, government should prefer forms of punishment that do *not* involve the drastic curtailment of liberty associated with imprisonment; in particular, it should prefer community service, probation, and electronic surveillance to imprisonment since this involves degradation while isolating people from everyday life. This isn't to say that incarceration is wholly out of the question; in particular, it isn't to say that prison must be abolished. Even when settling on incarceration, though, skepticism is in order as to the length of confinement—on the whole, the less, the better.

If followed, these proposals will substantially reduce incarceration, though they won't eliminate it entirely. The proposals are compatible with the current practice of plea bargaining—or at least they are as long as the compromise with *Miranda* noted in Chapter 7 is adopted. We should consider this point and then to another complicating factor that can be addressed through adoption of the proposals. As for *Miranda*, it was noted that few defense attorneys are willing to let their un-*Mirandized* clients talk to victims, thus making it unlikely that the restorative justice process will ever begin. The compromise proposed earlier accorded weight to the values associated with *Miranda* and also to those associated with restorative justice: make the defendant's statements during the conference conditional on his/her decision concerning the outcome of the discussion. Admittedly, this converts a confession into something inescapably transactional. On the other hand, it brings defendant and victim together to engage in a conversation that otherwise wouldn't happen. This factor outweighs others given the importance of reconciling grievances.[3]

In the sixth chapter, we noted the possibility of another issue that might complicate the process of taking accountability for one's conduct—or, at least, an issue with the potential for this if only courts would accord it more attention. This issue has to do with the untreated mental disorders of criminal defendants. As noted earlier, studies have shown that a substantial disproportion of convicted suffer from serious mental disorders.[4] This shortcoming has to be assessed in terms of the law's failure to provide a defendant with a psychiatrist of his/her own once the defendant raises a colorable claim of mental illness, for given findings about inmate mental disorders, it seems likely that many more people charged with crimes (and asked to account for their conduct) might plausibly rebuff ascriptions of responsibility on the ground that they were unable to regulate their behavior. A social justice deficit (undiagnosed mental illness) may undermine a social justice/criminal justice achievement, in other words (victim/offender reconciliation).

Their emphasis on accountability notwithstanding, commentators such as Michelle Alexander and Allegra McLeod don't address the complicating factors just mentioned. Those factors have been discussed here because a program of penal parsimony must deal with them if it's be deemed realistic and non-utopian. Plea bargaining is entrenched in the administration of criminal law. To expect it to disappear (or to retreat to silence about *Miranda's* repercussions) is to paint a false picture of the law's operation. Similarly, to fail to note the incidence of untreated mental illness among defendants is to disregard one social justice issue while focusing on another. The better approach is to think about what's been considered here—how different features of social justice can be integrated into the operation of a decent society's legal system.

The answer is that integration is awkward but feasible. Incorporating *Miranda* into the accountability process simultaneously enhances one social justice value while casting a shadow over the accountability process. Giving offenders an opportunity to examine their undiagnosed mental health problems is an essential element of social justice; it's likely to lead offenders to deny, or at least to deflect, responsibility for their harmful acts. But because both values matter, it's essential to reconcile them as best as possible in actual practice.

If we step back, we can imagine how the non-incarcerative policies outlined earlier might operate in actual cases. Think first about someone charged with financial fraud. Such a defendant would almost surely rely on *Miranda* as a shield against accountability. Only after confronting substantial evidence of guilt would this defendant make a (blatantly self-interested) decision to talk to his/her victims. The accountability process might begin here, for it's at this point that the offender would have to take seriously his/her victims' legitimate interests. At a minimum, he would have to talk to the victims about a restitution plan. Whether the victims would demand imprisonment is anyone's guess; it's clear, though, that electronic surveillance stands as an alternative to imprisonment in the context of this case.

Now consider a case of violence—aggravated assault by someone with a history of getting into fights with others. Here, too, the defendant might initially exercise his/her *Miranda* right. Consultation with a (state-provided) psychiatrist might lead the defendant to conclude that a restorative justice conference would be in order, though instead of apologizing the defendant might cite a disorder to account for the behavior. This explanation/non-apology might leave the victim dissatisfied. Assuming, though, that the official in charge of the case concludes that a psychiatrist has correctly identified a problem and prescribed a proper course of treatment (say, medication plus talk therapy) and that the defendant is willing to undertake the treatment, then imprisonment would be counterproductive.

Now consider a third case—an intentional killing during a lover's quarrel, with the defendant now overcome with remorse and prepared to apologize to his lover's family. *Miranda* doesn't stand in the way. Perhaps the lover's family isn't interested in punishment. But the culpability scale would come into play here, since murder is the crime at the top of the scale. Absent a reason for rebutting its pre-eminent position, an official would impose a term of imprisonment on the defendant. The term would almost certainly be substantially lower, though, than the top term in today's system.

Instead of just *leveling down*, then, sentencing in a decent society would *level down dramatically*. As the hypotheticals discussed above make clear, sentencing would still attend to the individualizing characteristics of specific cases. It would do so, however, by adhering to the spirit of penal parsimony, thereby showing respect for victims while also providing offenders with the leeway they need to repair their lives.

A milder version of penal parsimony In the long run, a decent society should take seriously the alternatives to incarceration just mentioned, for these offer a systemic solution to mass imprisonment while safeguarding the public. It might be argued, though, that the measures pose too much risk now—that is, it might be contended that the public safety uncertainties associated with novel sanctions are sufficiently serious to justify adoption of a *go slow* policy by testing them over time. This consideration of prudence must be borne in mind. But another point also merits consideration, which is that it's all too easy to overestimate dangers to public safety when thinking about imprisoning offenders (indeed, routine invocation of public safety risks during the late twentieth century played a major role in the dramatic increase in prison populations). The less drastic remedies examined in the remainder of this sub-section thus take the consideration of prudence into account without according it decisive weight. The remedies suggested offer a way to bring about a calibrated reduction in the prison population, in other words, one that takes seriously principles (i) to (iv) noted above but applying them less forcefully. These milder remedies do so in part by reducing prison-intake, in part by accelerating releases.

Consider first a remedy that could affect both intake and release: eliminating mandatory minimum sentences. These sentences affect intake because they require incarceration of offenders who might otherwise receive non-prison terms. They affect release because they require continued incarceration of offenders who pose a low risk of reoffending. Because both points matter, mandatory minimums should be rethought at the front *and* back ends—at the front through legislative reform that vests judges with discretion to set lower sentences and at the back by vesting parole boards with the discretion to modify sentences retroactively by relying on risk-assessment profiles for all inmates, particularly for elderly ones.

Now consider a straightforward intake strategy: redefining crimes, in particular by reclassifying felonies as misdemeanors. During the early 2010s, California, on confronting prison overcrowding that exceeded 125% of capacity, took this approach in what it called a realignment policy. Commenting on the policy's effect, Magnus Lofstrum and Brandon Martin concluded that it "significantly reduced the state's prison population" (though only after other initiatives contributed to this) and that it did so with no increase in violent crime.[5]

Another intake strategy involves rethinking mandatory imprisonment for probation and parole violations. The threat of imprisonment for either kind of violation may indeed play a necessary role in promoting compliance with the terms set by courts. Because it does, the threat of imprisonment for such violations shouldn't be wholly renounced. It can be modified, however. That is, if systematic risk-assessment is undertaken, intensive supervision short of imprisonment may work in many settings where violators pose little risk of violence, particularly in cases where a violator hasn't committed a crime.

In turning to strategies for accelerating prison-release, we encounter many different options. One has already been noted: retroactive cancellation of mandatory minimum sentences. Beyond this, two others have turned out to be especially helpful. One is conditional release prior to the announced end of a sentence, an option that's been implemented in Connecticut, Michigan, and Rhode Island. Another, which has been adopted in many states, combines adoption of a risk-assessment framework for those currently incarcerated along with reentry planning to supervise the transition from imprisonment to the outside world.[6]

When examined in isolation from one another, none of the front- or back-end strategies just mentioned will reduce dramatically the current rate of imprisonment. Taken together, though, they have the potential to bring about a substantial decrease in prison population. To use a phrase coined by Joan Petersilia and Francis Cullen, the strategies just outlined (plus others of a similar character) are "liberal but not stupid."[7] Moreover, if we add that a commitment to penal parsimony calls for experimentation with the more far-reaching remedies outlined earlier, in particular with restorative justice for a wide range of misdemeanors and low-level felonies and also extensive experimentation with electronic surveillance of convicted felons, we can anticipate a dramatic decrease in the prison population over a decade or so if they are adopted. Fewer people will enter prison; decarceration will accelerate; and the late twentieth century's addiction to imprisonment will gradually come to an end.

Social Justice Initiatives

These changes won't be long-lasting, however, absent an across-the-board commitment to social justice, one that extends beyond the administration of criminal law. In the long run, a decent society can't be sustained by threats of coercion. If such a society is to endure, it must rely on institutions that foster robust civic engagement. A decent society can't ignore criminal justice, in other words, but it must place primary emphasis on social justice.

Earlier chapters have distinguished between an ideal, a decent, and a problematic society. In thinking about social justice initiatives, we have a chance to consider this tripartite distinction in greater detail. An ideal society, it's been suggested, would be free of any acts of predation (in particular, it would not experience unprovoked violence and fraud)—and such a society thus wouldn't have to consider the possibility of criminal justice. In contrast, a decent society aims at something more modest—at promoting social justice while employing institutions that punish acts of predation. This goal is a realistic one,[8] and because it is, advocates of a decent society can reasonably insist on exceeding the minimal conditions outlined in earlier chapters—that is, they can insist not only on adoption of measures that minimize the influence of race and class in the distribution of burdens and benefits in social life, they can *also* insist on adoption of policies that promote the possibility of full equality of opportunity. To put this last point differently, advocates of a decent society can reasonably insist on the adoption of measures that correct the inequalities generated by the place of one's birth—they can aim, in other words, at overcoming zip code destiny. A decent society won't be one with equal outcomes. It will, however, be one that adopts policies that try to equalize the life chances of all its members.

What policies will be adopted and how will they be paid for? The chapter on white-collar crime provided a partial answer to the latter question when it examined ways in which government could pursue underpayment of taxes by wealthy members of society. In building on this, we can note that government must adopt other measures to increase tax revenues—that it not only must enforce the current tax code more vigorously but that it also must amend that code it in order to fund social justice initiatives. The initiatives outlined in the remainder of this chapter will require more revenue, in other words, than would currently be secured by existing taxes even if all these taxes were to be fully paid. In particular, the initiatives would require revenue from a wealth tax, one that taxes substantial fortunes at rates of 1 to 3% per annum. Such a tax would be doubly beneficial: it would reduce wealth inequality simply through its enforcement, and it would also provide revenue that could be deployed to enhance equitable terms of communal life.

And what initiatives should be taken? Three targets are essential, one involving children, another adolescents, and a third adults. As for children, research undertaken in recent years has established that investment in the earliest years of life produces greater returns (as measured in terms of equalizing life outcomes) than does investment in later years. Generalizing on this, James Heckman has identified a downward sloping curve, one in which early-childhood initiatives generate better results over time than do later ones. The Heckman curve is pertinent to all children.

(The Heckman Curve can be found at Table 6.) It's particularly relevant, though, to those born into at-risk settings—especially relevant, in other words, when thinking about the difficulties encountered by children born into the most impoverished zip codes. In examining a half-century's worth of programs that have intensively invested in services for children born into the poorest quartile of the population, Heckman has shown how positive results have emerged in all key features of life—in school-graduation rates, marital stability, and (of special importance here) crime-commission—by comparison with similarly situated children who didn't participate in such programs.[9] A decent society, we can say, *invests in kids*. It devotes as much in the way of resources, perhaps even more, to the first years of life as are now devoted to old age.

Investment in early childhood relies on a (wise) long-term strategy. A medium-range strategy is also essential, one that will have an immediate effect on crime rates as well as joblessness. This is to invest in a full-employment program for everyone above the age of 16. Researchers have established that crime rates decline when unemployment goes down.[10] The decline in crime has mostly been limited to property crime, it's been widely believed: It hasn't affected violence, and it's been weakest among adolescents, a group particularly prone to violence. Recent pilot programs suggest there's hope even here, however. Summer employment programs (that have recruited on a random basis and so can be studied from a control/experimental group perspective) run in Boston, New York, Philadelphia, and Chicago have produced violent crime reduction results among 14- to 21-year olds ranging from 10 to 33%. The beneficial effects have been long-lasting—that is, their participants' arrest records have continued at lower levels even after the programs have ended. If generalized, this suggests the possibility a general strategy that will complement the one Heckman advocates for young children: *invest in adolescents*, with the extra benefit that this will lead to a reduction in violent crime.[11]

Social-welfare programs (for health care, education, and housing, among others) are also key features of a decent society, and these matter for any age group or demographic. Of special importance, though, as we move along the spectrum of individual development is the possibility of meaningful employment for every adult capable of work. The complement to comprehensive investment in childhood, in other words, is government investment in employment opportunities for every person of adult age. Employment opportunities are distinguishable from welfare benefits. The latter are best understood as the floor of social decency;

they're provided directly by government. The former define its full meaning; they're best provided by the private sector, but government can actively involve itself in overseeing labor markets so as to generate full employment. This point is critically important wholly apart from questions about crime rates. It takes on particular urgency, though, because unemployment and underemployment are breeding grounds for crime. A recent econometric study of the Brazilian economy, for instance, suggests that mass layoffs produce a substantial increase in crime, with this increase concentrated among those who have recently been hired. A social justice policy of full employment can contribute to crime reduction, in other words.[12]

Because discussion in this chapter (and throughout the entire book) has not focused on the possibility of an ideal setting in which human predation disappears, it's avoided utopian reasoning about crime-free communities. The chapter's comments on penal parsimony still matter apart from its comments on social justice initiatives, then, for violations of the obligations of restraint, it can reasonably be expected, will (and perhaps will forever) remain a recurrent feature of social life. On the other hand, a socially just society is likely to reduce the occurrence of these violations—and this benefit will be a welcome one for all involved.

Notes

1. For analysis, see The Sentencing Project, *Growth in Mass Incarceration* (2024) @ sentencingproject.org/research.
2. Norval Morris, *The Future of Imprisonment* 61–62 (1974).
3. This follows the proposal for conditional *Miranda* waiver in the context of a restorative justice conference. See *supra* note 16 in Chapter 6 and accompanying text.
4. For a summary of research, see Prison Policy Institute, *Mental Health* (2024) @ https://prisonpolicy.org/research/mental_health/
5. Magnus Lofstrum and Brandon Martin, "Public Safety Realignment: The Impacts So Far," *Public Policy Institute of California* (2015) @ ppic.org/publication/public-safety-realignments-so-far.
6. For discussion, see Peggy Burke, "TPC Reentry Handbook: Implementing the NIC Transition from Prison to the Community Model," *National Institute of Correction Library Collection* (2008).

7. Joan Petersilia and Francis Cullen, "Liberal but not Stupid: Meeting the Promise of Prison Downsizing," *Stanford Review of Law and Policy* 2: 1 (2015).
8. Because the framework outlined here is non-utopian, it's to be distinguished from what Rawls called his "realistic utopia." See, Rawls, *supra* note 7 in Introduction.
9. For further discussion, see James Heckman, *Giving Kids a Fair Chance* (2013).
10. See Steven Raphael and Rudolf Winter-Ebmer, "Identifying the Effect of Unemployment on Crime," *The Journal of Law and Economics* 44: 259 (2001).
11. For further discussion, see Jonathan Davis and Sara Heller, "Rethinking the Benefits of Youth Employment Programs: The Heterogeneous Effects of Summer Jobs," *The Review of Economics and Statistics* 102: 664 (2020).
12. See Diogio Britto et al., "The Effect of Job Loss and Unemployment Insurance on Crime in Brazil," *Econometrica* 90: 1393 (2022). See generally Raphael and Winter-Ebmer, *supra* note 10.

Conclusion: Mandela's Role Reversal Revisited

In returning to Mandela's role reversal, we can say, by way of conclusion, that the government should *always* be in the dock when it initiates criminal charges. This is because wariness is invariably in order as far as the administration of criminal law is concerned. The criminal process typically begins with an act of domination (with an arrest followed by a search of the arrestee's person). It continues with more sustained acts of domination (including imprisonment following conviction). If, as suggested throughout this book, the word *justice* refers to the master concept used for thinking about the fair terms of cooperation free and equal people would adopt for living together, then of course wariness is in order at every stage of the criminal process, for the domination essential to effective administration of the criminal law can be justified only by showing that it doesn't exceed the minimum necessary for implementing practices that, apart from the contribution they make to vindication of the obligations of restraint, would be rejected as profoundly *un*just.

Mandela would surely have agreed with this point. The plea he entered at his 1963 trial suggested something more, however. It suggested that a special degree of suspicion is in order because the state may deploy its penal power for pathological purposes—that an extra layer of suspicion is needed not merely because individual state officials may act as thuggish rogues but also because state penal power can be deployed in a systematically oppressive way to promote racial and class domination. Mandela's plea pertained to South African apartheid. The preceding chapters have

W. C. Heffernan, *Social Justice/Criminal Justice*,
https://doi.org/10.1007/978-3-031-75397-8

generalized on it—that is, they've suggested that there's always a possibility government may use its coercive power pathologically and that, given this systemic threat, it's essential to consider carefully the possibility that criminal law is being deployed to promote social injustice.

The preceding chapters have advanced a further argument as well. Even when government adopts constitutional rules that commit it to eradication of the vestiges of the past—even when it aims at establishing the institutions essential to a decent society (i.e., institutions that distribute resources and opportunities fairly and that resolve grievances impartially)—it's critical to ask whether the legal commitments made are being honored in practice. The chapters in the book's later sections provide evidence to believe that commitments made as a matter of American constitutional law are routinely not honored by the country's officials in the daily administration of criminal law. Racial disparities persist in policing and in the imposition of punishment. Class disparities persist as far as bail and access to counsel are concerned. Furthermore, because of funding shortfalls, a substantial amount of white-collar crime is either uninvestigated or underprosecuted. Given these shortcomings, the earlier chapters have suggested, current practice is problematic: it falls short of minimal decency because race and class continue to figure so prominently in outcomes of the criminal process.

A minimally decent society, the book has argued, would eliminate the influence of race and class in the everyday operation of the criminal process. It would adopt remedial measures to address bias in police use of force; it would make sure class disparities don't disrupt access to bail and legal counsel; and it would oversee sentencing to ensure that racial factors don't distort the imposition of punishment. Moreover, a minimally decent society wouldn't punish people for mere possession of mind-altering substances, and such a society also would adopt measures to ensure that its prosperous members can't use their advantages to avoid punishment for acts of fraud.

A wholly decent society would aim at something more, the book has contended. It would adopt social justice initiatives to promote the possibility of equal life chances for all citizens—and, in doing so, it would reduce the likelihood of crime itself. At no time has it been suggested that there is a reasonable prospect of eliminating criminal activity (and thus of eliminating punishment) altogether. Predatory aggression against others—not merely violence but also fraud—has long been a feature of the human condition. It's utopian to expect that this will disappear entirely.

It's realistic, however, to aim at substantial crime reduction through sustained social justice initiatives that equalize resources and opportunities. Such initiatives are worthwhile in themselves—that is, they're intrinsically desirable because they can promote fair terms of cooperation in everyday life. But they're also worth adopting because they can make law enforcement a less important component of communal life. It's by reasoning in terms of this conception of social decency—not merely the minimal decency that addresses disparities in the administration of criminal law but fully realized decency throughout the community—that the coercive power of the state can be tamed even it can't be eliminated.

Appendix

W. C. Heffernan, *Social Justice/Criminal Justice*,
https://doi.org/10.1007/978-3-031-75397-8

Table A1 Stop, question, and frisk under three twenty-first-century New York City Mayors

Mayor	*Year*	*Index crimes*	*Interventions*				*Nothing Found*	*Hit rate*				*Percentage of those stopped suspected of carrying a weapon or contraband*			*Hit rate (among those suspected for carrying a weapon/ contraband)*		
			Total	*White*	*Black*	*Hispanic*		*Overall (%)*	*White (%)*	*Black (%)*	*Hispanic (%)*	*White (%)*	*Black (%)*	*Hispanic (%)*	*White (%)*	*Black (%)*	*Hispanic (%)*
Bloomberg	2003	236,215	160,851	17,623	77,704	44,581	140,442	13.0	10.6	12.4	13.7	8.6	12.8	11.8	10.4	6.9	9.2
	2004	226,876	313,523	28,913	155,030	89,936	278,933	11.0	11.8	11.1	11.6	8.5	13.2	11.1	10.4	5.8	8.1
	2005	217,132	398,191	40,713	196,568	115,088	352,348	11.0	11.6	11.9	11.5	7.7	13.1	11.3	9.9	5.0	6.2
	2006	205,522	506,491	53,496	267,450	147,852	457.163	10.0	10.3	9.6	10.2	7.0	12.4	11.7	6.3	2.6	3.1
	2007	199,941	472,096	52,887	243,756	141,864	410,936	13.0	12.9	12.9	13.3	7.3	13.7	12.6	7.9	3.7	4.1
	2008	198,319	540,302	57,650	275,588	168,474	474,387	12.0	11.2	12.2	12.7	7.4	13.3	12.8	16.0	6.0	7.3
	2009	188,357	581,168	53,601	310,611	180,055	510,742	12.0	11.9	11.9	12.7	7.8	13.4	12.1	18.1	5.7	7.8
	2010	188,104	601,285	54,810	315,083	189,326	518,849	14.0	13.6	13.4	14.3	8.1	11.8	11.1	20.5	6.4	8.9
	2011	191,666	685,724	61,805	350,743	223,740	605,328	12.0	13.1	11.5	11.8	7.2	11.0	10.5	19.2	6.3	7.4
	2012	195,753	532,911	50,366	284,229	165,140	473,644	11.0	11.6	10.5	12.0	7.4	10.1	10.3	21.5	6.9	9.2
	2013	194,355	191,851	20,820	104,449	54,930	169,252	12.0	11.9	10.5	13.3	8.0	11.4	11.1	22.4	9.1	13.2
de Blasio	2014	185,191	45,787	5467	24,319	12,489	37,744	18.0	15.9	16.5	21.6	7.8	8.2	9.1	30.8	13.7	20.0
	2015	179,948	22,565	2514	11,950	6499	18,353	20.0	16.0	19.1	24.2	9.5	11.3	12.4	34.3	22.2	27.2
	2016	174,402	12,404	1270	6498	3626	9394	24.0	23.5	23.1	27.9	9.0	10.2	9.8	35.1	22.1	33.6
	2017	171,248	11,629	977	6595	3567	7833	33.0	38.0	31.0	35.5	11.6	18.3	17.3	52.2	38.9	46.3
	2018	174,164	11,008	1074	6241	3389	7645	30.0	30.4	29.7	32.7	10.7	19.8	16.0	32.2	34.1	38.8

Mayor	*Year*	*Index crimes*	*Interventions*				*Nothing Found*	*Hit rate*				*Percentage of those stopped suspected of carrying a weapon or contraband*			*Hit rate (among those suspected for carrying a weapon/ contraband)*		
			Total	*White*	*Black*	*Hispanic*		*Overall (%)*	*White (%)*	*Black (%)*	*Hispanic (%)*	*White (%)*	*Black (%)*	*Hispanic (%)*	*White (%)*	*Black (%)*	*Hispanic (%)*
	2019	170,120	13,459	1215	7981	3869	8867	34.0	36.1	33.6	35.1	9.6	20.4	19.7	35.9	33.8	37.5
	2020	177,319	9543	856	5366	2879	7670	19.63	15.8	19.9	20.1	9.9	21.1	18.2	44.7	45.7	47.0
	2021	186,505	8947	732	5404	2457	7115	20.48	16.8	21.5	20.4	9.0	30.9	24.3	51.5	39.7	43.0
Adams	2022	237,654	15,102	1077	8863	4477	12,012	20.46	14.9	21.1	21.0	12.0	39.9	35.9	33.3	34.3	35.1
	2023		16,971	942	9939	5166	13,693	19.32	12.2	19.8	20.0	14.4	49.6	46.4	20.6	28.2	28.7

Sources Index Crime: New York State Division of Criminal Justice Services, "New York State Index Crime Data Table."
SQF Interventions: New York Police Department, "Stop, Question, and Frisk Database," 2003–2023. Race is based on officer-reported suspect race. Hit rate is calculated based on whether a pistol, a rifle, a machine gun, an assault weapon, a knife or a cutting instrument, or any other kind of weapon or contraband was found on the suspect. Suspicion for carrying a weapon or contraband is based on whether the officers' reported reasons for the stop include carrying a suspicious object or having a suspicious bulge.

Table A2 Racial and gender disparities in federal non-capital sentencing

Year	*Average prison sentence (in months)*					
	Black female	*Black male*	*Hispanic female*	*Hispanic male*	*White female*	*White male*
1999	41.7	86.9	31.1	44.0	27.7	50.5
2000	36.6	87.7	28.9	42.7	29.0	50.3
2001	33.0	84.8	28.8	42.6	30.0	51.9
2002	24.6	84.5	30.4	42.3	32.1	52.5
2003	35.3	89.1	29.1	41.8	34.6	57.3
2004	37.6	90.5	29.3	43.6	37.6	60.3
2005	37.2	91.4	29.1	43.4	37.5	60.5
2006	37.9	89.3	30.3	44.9	37.5	64.2
2007	39.9	93.7	28.7	44.6	39.0	64.1
2008	22.8	84.5	25.9	40.5	24.6	50.3
2009	24.9	84.0	22.6	37.0	24.3	49.2
2010	24.1	79.7	22.0	35.8	25.7	50.3
2011	22.5	77.0	21.8	34.5	25.5	50.6
2012	23.7	74.3	24.7	36.4	27.3	51.9
2013	23.7	74.3	24.7	36.4	27.3	51.9
2014	23.4	72.2	20.3	33.3	28.0	55.6
2015	22.2	67.9	20.9	32.1	26.5	55.2
2016	19.5	66.7	21.2	30.9	29.2	58.2
2017	20.9	68.0	22.7	31.2	32.7	60.0
2018	22.1	69.8	21.6	28.7	36.4	64.6
2019	24.1	69.5	20.9	26.2	36.9	65.3
2020	34.2	73.1	23.4	24.3	51.1	73.8

Year	*Average prison sentence (in months)*					
	Black female	*Black male*	*Hispanic female*	*Hispanic male*	*White female*	*White male*
2021	31.0	71.5	30.1	34.1	49.8	76.9
2022	34.8	74.8	28.4	36.6	50.8	78.5

Source United States Sentencing Commission Data File, 1999–2022. Average prison sentence includes time imposed, time served, and §5G1.3 credits (SENTTOT). Variables used to categorize race and gender: MONSEX and NEWRACE.

Table A3 Vestiges of Jim Crow in the administration of the death penalty: The Baldus pattern in North Carolina

	Black defendant-White victim		*White defendant-White victim*		*Black defendant-Black victim*		*White defendant-Black victim*	
	1930–1940	*1990–2009*	*1930–1940*	*1990–2009*	*1930–1940*	*1990–2009*	*1930–1940*	*1990–2009*
Death-Eligible Cases	51	270	165	475	581	580	24	43
Convicted on Death-Eligible Murder	35	156	59	248	223	200	7	21
% of Eligible Cases	68.7%	57.8%	35.8%	52.2%	38.4%	38.5%	29.2%	48.8%
# of Death Sentences	15	68	11	129	15	85	0	5
% of Convicted Cases	42.8%	43.6%	18.6%	52.0%	6.7%	42.5%	0.0%	23.8%

Sources: 1930–1940: Harold Garfinkel, "Research Note on Inter- and Intra-Racial Homicides," *Social Forces*, Vol. 27, No. 4 (May, 1949), pp. 369–381. Death eligible cases are from Table 1; data on convictions and death sentences are from Table 7. All cases are homicide incidents, not including rape.
1990–2009: Barbara O'Brien, Catherine Grosso, George Woodworth, and Abijah Taylor, "Untangling the Role of Race in Capital Charging and Sentencing in North Carolina, 1990–2009," *North Carolina Law Review*, Vol. 97, No. 6 (September, 2016). Eligible, convicted, and imposed cases are from Table 1.

Table A4 Average sentence length (in months) for violent crimes and white-collar crimes in federal courts, 2006–2023

Year	*Violent offenses*		*White-Collar offenses*		*Ratio*	
	Average sentence length	*Number of cases*	*Average sentence length*	*Number of cases*	*Average sentence length*	*Number of cases*
2006	77.4	12,162	18.9	10,189	4.1: 1	1.2: 1
2007	79.0	12,419	19.3	10,512	4.1: 1	1.2: 1
2008	80.1	12,085	21.1	10,709	3.8: 1	1.1: 1
2009	82.1	12,208	21.2	10,613	3.9: 1	1.2: 1
2010	85.9	12,927	21.9	11,093	3.9: 1	1.2: 1
2011	86.1	12,763	22.0	11,416	3.9: 1	1.1: 1
2012	87.9	13,238	23.2	11,515	3.8: 1	1.1: 1
2013	88.4	13,238	24.9	11,515	3.6: 1	1.1: 1
2014	88.3	12,947	25.3	10,456	3.5: 1	1.2: 1
2015	88.5	12,206	25.2	9735	3.5: 1	1.3: 1
2016	85.7	12,368	23.6	8753	3.6: 1	1.4: 1
2017	83.1	13,010	24.4	8094	3.4: 1	1.6: 1
2018	80.2	12,736	27.3	9162	2.9: 1	1.4: 1
2019	78.9	13,885	25.9	8751	3.0: 1	1.6: 1
2020	68.6	11,519	31.4	6518	2.2: 1	1.8: 1
2021	67.5	12,466	34.7	6410	1.9: 1	1.9: 1
2022	71.2	14,391	34.6	7687	2.1: 1	1.9: 1
2023	72.3	14,102	28.6	7459	2.5: 1	1.9: 1

Sources 2006–2022: United States Sentencing Commission Data File, 2006–2022; Violent offenses include assault, arson, child pornography, firearm offenses, kidnapping, manslaughter, murder, prison offenses, racketeering, and robbery; white-collar offenses include antitrust, bribery, embezzlement, fraud, forgery, money laundering, and tax offenses. Variables used to identify offenses: OFFGUIDE and OFFTYPE2. Sentence lengths are average prison sentences, including time imposed, time served, and §5G1.3 credits (variable: SENTTOT).
2023: United States Sentencing Commission, "Quarterly Data Report," Fiscal Year 2023, Table 6.

Table A5 The trajectory of mass incarceration over the last half-century, 1978–2021

Year	*Prison population under Federal and State Jurisdiction*	*Number of inmates held in local jail*	*Number of probationers*	*Number of homicides*	*Prison admissions*	*Prison admission to homicide ratio*	*Prison population in England and Wales*	*Homicides in England and Wales*	*Prisoner to homicide ratio*	
									U.S	*England and Wales*
1978	294,396		905,652	19,560	152,039	7.8	41,796	536	15.1: 1	78.0: 1
1979	301,470		1,086,535	21,460	161,280	7.5	42,220	620	14.0: 1	68.1: 1
1980	315,974		1,118,097	23,040	171,884	7.5	42,264	626	13.7: 1	67.5: 1
1981	353,673		1,222,024	22,520	199,943	8.9	43,311	556	15.7: 1	77.9: 1
1982	395,516		1,335,359	21,010	218,087	10.4	43,707	618	18.8: 1	70.7: 1
1983	419,346		1,502,247	19,308	237,925	12.3	43,462	552	21.7: 1	78.7: 1
1984	443,398		1,740,948	18,692	234,293	12.5	43,295	619	23.7: 1	69.9: 1
1985	480,568	256,615	1,870,132	17,546	258,514	14.7	46,233	625	27.4: 1	74.0: 1
1986	522,084		2,114,821	19,269	291,903	15.1	46,770	659	27.1: 1	71.0: 1
1987	560,812		2,242,053	17,967	326,228	18.2	48,426	687	31.2: 1	70.5: 1
1988	603,732		2,356,483	17,977	365,724	20.3	48,872	645	33.6: 1	75.8: 1
1989	680,907		2,521,525	18,960	447,388	23.6	48,500	622	35.9: 1	78.0: 1
1990	739,980	405,320	2,670,234	20,278	462,500	22.8	44,975	661	36.5: 1	68.0: 1
1991	789,612	426,479		21,690	468,000	21.6	44,809	725	36.4: 1	61.8: 1
1992	846,277	444,584		22,726	482,400	21.2	44,719	681	37.2: 1	65.7: 1
1993	932,074	459,804		23,182	500,335	21.6	44,552	674	40.2: 1	66.1: 1
1994	1,016,690	486,474		22,096	523,577	23.7	48,621	728	46.0: 1	66.8: 1
1995	1,085,020	507,044	3,077,861	20,231	549,313	27.2	50,962	752	53.6: 1	67.8: 1
1996	1,137,722	518,492	3,164,996	16,974	542,863	32.0	55,281	676	67.0: 1	81.8: 1
1997	1,194,334	567,079	3,296,513	15,847	572,281	36.1	61,114	734	75.4: 1	83.3: 1
1998	1,256,474	592,462	3,417,613	14,213	603,510	42.5	65,298	728	88.4: 1	89.7: 1
1999	1,304,081	605,943	3,779,922	13,019	606,728	46.6	64,771	741	100.2: 1	87.4: 1

Year	*Prison population under Federal and State Jurisdiction*	*Number of inmates held in local jail*	*Number of probationers*	*Number of homicides*	*Prison admissions*	*Prison admission to homicide ratio*	*Prison population in England and Wales*	*Homicides in England and Wales*	*Prisoner to homicide ratio*	
									U.S	*England and Wales*
2000	1,334,174	621,149	3,839,532	13,232	654,534	49.5	64,602	761	100.8: 1	84.9: 1
2001	1,345,217	631,240	3,931,731	14,087	638,978	45.4	66,301	847	95.5: 1	78.3: 1
2002	1,380,516	665,475	3,995,165	14,279	660,576	46.3	71,218	857	96.7: 1	83.1: 1
2003	1,408,361	691,301	4,024,067	14,457	686,471	47.5	73,657	1,043	97.4: 1	70.6: 1
2004	1,433,728	713,990	4,120,012	14,248	697,066	48.9	74,488	857	100.6: 1	86.9: 1
2005	1,462,866	747,529	4,143,792	14,990	730,141	48.7	76,190	833	97.6: 1	91.5: 1
2006	1,504,598	766,010	4,237,023	15,103	747,031	49.5	77,982	767	99.6: 1	101.7: 1
2007	1,532,851	780,174	4,293,163	14,928	742,875	49.8	79,734	752	102.7: 1	106.0: 1
2008	1,547,742	785,533	4,270,917	14,305	738,631	51.6	83,194	774	108.2: 1	107.5: 1
2009	1,553,574	767,434	4,203,967	13,764	728,686	52.9	83,391	672	112.9: 1	124.1: 1
2010	1,552,669	748,728	4,055,514	13,188	703,798	53.4	85,002	623	117.7: 1	136.4: 1
2011	1,538,847	735,600	3,973,800	12,810	671,551	52.4	85,374	655	120.1: 1	130.3: 1
2012	1,512,430	744,500	3,944,900	12,992	609,781	46.9	86,048	545	116.4: 1	157.9: 1
2013	1,520,403	731,200	3,912,900	12,412	608,442	49.0	83,842	567	122.5: 1	147.9: 1
2014	1,507,781	744,600	3,868,400	12,281	631,168	51.4	85,509	539	122.8: 1	158.6: 1
2015	1,476,847	728,200	3,789,800	13,783	608,318	44.1	86,193	526	107.1: 1	163.9: 1
2016	1,459,948	740,700	3,673,100	15,320	606,000	39.6	85,134	556	95.3: 1	153.1: 1
2017	1,439,877	745,200	3,647,200	15,312	606,571	39.6	85,863	707	94.0: 1	121.4: 1
2018	1,413,370	738,400	3,540,000	14,605	596,407	40.8	82,773	718	96.8: 1	115.3: 1
2019	1,379,786	734,500	3,492,900	14,678	576,956	39.3	82,710	655	94.0: 1	126.3: 1

(continued)

Table A5 (continued)

Year	*Prison population under Federal and State Jurisdiction*	*Number of inmates held in local jail*	*Number of probationers*	*Number of homicides*	*Prison admissions*	*Prison admission to homicide ratio*	*Prison population in England and Wales*	*Homicides in England and Wales*	*Prisoner to homicide ratio*	
									U.S	*England and Wales*
2020	1,185,733	549,100	3,053,700	18,965	346,461	18.3	79,514	689	62.5: 1	115.4: 1
2021	1,163,665	636,300	2,963,000	16,413	421,006	25.7	78,324	568	70.9: 1	137.9: 1

Sources Prison Population: The Sentencing Project, "Mass Incarceration Trends", 2024, Fig. 1.

Jail and Probation Population: Bureau of Justice Statistics, "Prison and Jail Inmates 1995" and subsequent annual reports in the "Prison and Jail Inmates at Midyear" series from 1996–2021 (jail population are estimated as the number of inmates held on the last weekday in June); Bureau of Justice Statistics, "Probation and Parole in the United States, 1979" and subsequent reports in the "Probation and Parole Populations" series from 1981–1988, 1990, and 1998–2021.

Prison Admission: Bureau of Justice Statistics, "Prisoners in 2012: Trends in Admissions and Releases, 1991–2012" and subsequent annual reports in the "Prisoners" series from 2013 through 2021.

Homicides in the U.S.: Federal Bureau of Investigation Crime Data Explorer, Expanded Homicide Data, 1985–2021; Bureau of Justice Statistics, "Homicide in the U.S. Known to Law Enforcement, 2011."

Prison Population in England and Wales: House of Commons Library, "UK Prison Population Statistics," 2023.

Homicides in England and Wales: Office for National Statistics, "Homicide in England and Wales: year ending March 2023."

Table A6 The Heckman Curve

	Treatment group	*Control group*
Education Outcomes		
Enrolled in special education program	15%	34%
Scored above 10th percentile in CAT	49%	15%
Graduated high school on-time	66%	45%
Economic Activities through Age 40		
Earn > $2,000 monthly	29%	7%
Own a Home	36%	13%
Not on welfare as an adult	29%	14%
Criminal Activities Involvement		
Number of Violent Misdemeanor Convictions		
at 30	0.05	0.52
at 40	0.09	0.68
at 50	0.15	0.72
Number of Violent Felony Convictions		
at 30	0.19	0.28
at 40	0.19	0.48
at 50	0.21	0.64

Source James Heckman, *Giving Kids a Fair Chance*, MIT Press, 2013

Index

W. C. Heffernan, *Social Justice/Criminal Justice*,
https://doi.org/10.1007/978-3-031-75397-8

SPRINGER NATURE

GPSR Compliance

The European Union's (EU) General Product Safety Regulation (GPSR) is a set of rules that requires consumer products to be safe and our obligations to ensure this.

If you have any concerns about our products, you can contact us on ProductSafety@springernature.com

In case Publisher is established outside the EU, the EU authorized representative is:

Springer Nature Customer Service Center GmbH
Europaplatz 3
69115 Heidelberg, Germany

The manufacturer's authorised representative in the EU is Springer Nature Customer Service Centre GmbH, Europaplatz 3, 69115 Heidelberg, Germany. If you have any concerns regarding our products, please contact ProductSafety@springernature.com

Printed and bound by CPI Group (UK) Ltd, Croydon, CR0 4YY
01/10/2026
02225978-0015